Studies in Middle-Assyrian Chronology and Religion

The publication of this book was made possible through a gift by SIDNEY NEUMANN, of Philadelphia, in memory of his parents, ABRAHAM and EMMA NEUMANN.

Studies in Middle-Assyrian Chronology and Religion

BY

HILLEL A. FINE, M.H.L., Ph.D.
Assistant Professor of Bible and Semitic Languages,
Hebrew Union College - Jewish Institute of Religion, Cincinnati

WIPF & STOCK · Eugene, Oregon

Wipf and Stock Publishers
199 W 8th Ave, Suite 3
Eugene, OR 97401

Studies in Middle-Assyrian Chronology and Religion
By Fine, Hillel A.
Softcover ISBN-13: 978-1-6667-5538-1
Hardcover ISBN-13: 978-1-6667-5539-8
eBook ISBN-13: 978-1-6667-5540-4
Publication date 8/3/2022
Previously published by Hebrew Union College Press, 1955

This edition is a scanned facsimile of the original edition published in 1955.

These studies were originally published in *HUCA*, Volumes XXIV and XXV. For the sake of convenience in reference to these volumes, the original pagination has been retained. Pages 1–88 are the equivalent of *HUCA*, XXIV, pages 187–273. Pages 89–151 are the equivalent of *HUCA* XXV, pages 107–168

Table of Contents

PAGE

List of Chronological and Genealogical Tables ix

List of Abbreviations xi

Introduction 1

Chapter I 3
The Fifteenth Century

Chapter II 8
The Fourteenth Century

Chapter III 42
The Thirteenth Century

Chapter IV 89
The Rule of Ninurta-tukulti-Aššur

Chapter V 98
Some Aspects of Assyrian Religion

Appendix 117
Corrections to Ebeling's *Eigennamen*

Index. . . . 147

List of Chronological and Genealogical Tables

		PAGE
I.	Documents and Eponymies of the Fifteenth Century	7
II.	The Genealogy of Labunii̯a	10
III	The Genealogy of Nûr-Kubi	34
IV.	Documents and Eponymies of the Fourteenth Century	38
V.	Documents and Eponymies of the Thirteenth Century	79
VI.	The Frequency of the Theophorous Elements in Middle-Assyrian Names	98
VII.	The Principal Merchants and Officials of the Middle-Assyrian Business and Juridical Documents.	145

List of Abbreviations

AfO	*Archiv fur Orientforschung*
AK	*Archiv fur Keilschriftforschung*
AKA	Budge, E. A., and King, L. W., *Annals of the Kings of Assyria*, London, 1902
Andrae, *Fest.*	Andrae, W., *Die Festungswerke von Assur* (Wissenschaftliche Veröffentlichung der Deutschen Orient-Gesellschaft, No. 23), Leipzig, 1913
AO	*Archiv Orientální*
AOB (I)	*Altorientalische Bibliothek* (Vol I, Ebeling, E., *Die Inschriften der altassyrischen Konige*, Leipzig, 1926)
Bi	Texts quoted by Speiser, E. A., "Gleanings from the Billa Texts," *Koschaker Festschrift*, pp. 141 ff.
CH	Ungnad, A., *Keilschrifttexte der Gesetze Ḫammurapis*, Leipzig 1909
Clay	Clay, A. T., *Personal Names from Cuneiform Inscriptions of the Cassite Period* (Yale Oriental Series, vol. 1), New Haven, 1912
CT XXXIII; XXXIV	*Cuneiform Texts from Babylonian Tablets in the British Museum*, parts XXXIII and XXXIV, London, 1912 and 1914
Ebeling, *Eigennamen*	Ebeling, E., *Die Eigennamen der mittelassyrischen Rechts- und Geschaftsurkunden* (*MAOG*, vol. XIII, part 1), Leipzig, 1939
Ebeling, *Urkunden*	Ebeling, E., *Urkunden des Archivs von Assur* (*MAOG*, vol VII, parts 1 and 2), Leipzig, 1933
Eigennamen	*See* Ebeling, *Eigennamen*
GPM	Gelb, I. J., Purves, P. M., and MacRae, A. A., *Nuzi Personal Names* (University of Chicago, *Oriental Institute Publications*, volume LVII), Chicago, 1943
HUCA	*Hebrew Union College Annual*

HWB	Delitzsch, F., *Assyrisches Handworterbuch*, Leipzig, 1896
JNES	*Journal of Near Eastern Studies*
KAH I, II	Messerschmidt, L. (volume 1), and Schroeder, O. (volume 2), *Keilschrifttexte aus Assur historischen Inhalts*, Leipzig, 1911, 1922
KAJ	Ebeling, E., *Keilschrifttexte aus Assur juristischen Inhalts*, Leipzig, 1927
KAV	Schroeder, O., *Keilschrifttexte aus Assur verschiedenen Inhalts*, Leipzig, 1920
KUB IV	*Keilschrifturkunden aus Boghazkoj*, volume IV, Berlin, 1922
Lewy, *KTS*	Lewy, J , *Die altassyrischen Texte vom Kultepe* (*Keilschrifttexte in den Antiken-Museen zu Stambul*), Constantinople, 1926
Lewy, *Tanis Bead*	Lewy J , "The Middle Assyrian Votive Bead Found at Tanis," *Ignace Goldziher Memorial Volume*, Part I, pp. 313–327, Budapest, 1948
Liverpool Annals	University of Liverpool, *Annals of Archaeology and Anthropology*
MAOG	*Mitteilungen der Altorientalischen Gesellschaft*
Meyer	Meyer, E., *Geschichte des Altertums*, Stuttgart, 1921
Muller, *Ass Rit.*	Muller, K. F , *Das Assyrische Ritual*, Teil I, *Texte zum Assyrischen Konigsritual* (*MVAeG*, vol. XLI, part 3), Leipzig, 1937
Muss-Arnolt	Muss-Arnolt, W., *Assyrisch-Englisch-Deutsches Handworterbuch*, Berlin, 1905
MVAG (*MVAeG*)	*Mitteilungen der Vorderasiatischen* (*Vorderasiatisch-Aegyptischen*) *Gesellschaft*
NRU	Koschaker, P., "Neue keilschriftliche Rechtsurkunden aus der El-Amarna Zeit" (*Abhandlungen der philologisch-historischen Klasse der sachsischen Akademie der Wissenschaft*, vol. XXXIX, no. 5), Leipzig, 1928
OLZ	*Orientalistische Literaturzeitung*
RA	*Revue d'Assyriologie*
RLA	*Reallexikon der Assyriologie*

SO	*Studia Orientalia*
Speleers	Speleers, L., *Recueil des Inscriptions de l'Asie Antérieure des Musées Royaux du Cinquantenaire à Bruxelles*, 1925
Stamm	Stamm, J. J., *Die Akkadische Namengebung* (*MVAeG*, vol. XLIV), Leipzig, 1939
Stephens	Stephens, F. J., *Personal Names from Cuneiform Inscriptions of Cappadocia* (*Yale Oriental Series, Researches*, vol. XIII), New Haven, 1928
Symbolae Koschaker	*Symbolae ad iura orientis antiqui pertinentes, Paulo Koschaker dedicatae*, Leiden, 1939
Synchr. Hist.	"The Synchronistic History," quoted according to the edition of *CT* XXXIV, Plates 38 ff.
Tallqvist, *Gotterep.*	Tallqvist, K., *Akkadische Gotterepitheta*, *SO* VII, Helsingfors, 1938
Urkunden	*See* Ebeling, *Urkunden*
W. 50–	Texts published in transliteration by Weidner, E. F., "Aus den Tagen eines assyrischen Schattenkönigs," *AfO* X, pp. 1–52
Waterman	Waterman, L., *Royal Correspondence of the Assyrian Empire* (University of Michigan, *Humanistic Series*, volumes XVII–XX), Ann Arbor, 1930–36
Weidner, *Studien zur Chron.*	Weidner, E. F , *Studien zur assyrisch-babylonischen Chronologie und Geschichte*, *MVAG* 1915, part 4, Leipzig, 1917
Weidner, *Konige von Assyrien*	Weidner, E. F , *Die Konige von Assyrien*, *MVAG* 1921, part 2, Leipzig, 1921
Winckler	Winckler, H., *Altorientalische Forschungen* Dritte Reihe, Band II, 3, Leipzig, 1905
YBT	*Yale Oriental Series, Babylonian Texts*
ZA	*Zeitschrift fur Assyriologie*

Studies in Middle-Assyrian Chronology and Religion

STUDIES IN MIDDLE-ASSYRIAN CHRONOLOGY AND RELIGION

PART I

INTRODUCTION

ACCORDING to Weidner,[1] Tukulti-Ninurta I's conquest of Babylon (1240 B. C.) entailed, to some extent, a victory for the Babylonian culture over that of the conqueror. The image of Marduk was captured and brought to Assyria, but for many, its presence symbolized an older and richer civilization, which exerted a growing fascination among them

There is not much direct evidence of this Babylonian influence within the Assyrian empire. Weidner points to the rivalry between king and nobles, and to the murder of the king, presumably by those who resented his religious innovations. The most specific evidence, however, is said to lie in the increasing use of the element "*Marduk*" in Assyrian theophorous names; and Weidner quotes a number of such names from this general period as evidence of his contention. To be sure, he himself admits the precarious nature of such proof. Nevertheless, the presence of these names at least makes it clear, that the cult of Marduk had its Assyrian adherents in the time of Tukulti-Ninurta.

Unfortunately, Weidner's evidence shows little more than this. Whether the frequency of such names in the reign of Tukulti-Ninurta was significantly higher than in previous years, Weidner was not ready to determine. The chronology of the Middle-Assyrian business documents, from which most of these names are culled, had not been established sufficiently for his hypothesis to be proved on a statistical basis.

[1] *AfO*, XIII, pp 119 ff

There had been a few attempts to discover the date of a; number of these tablets. Koschaker[2] had dealt with some of them, but in the course of his study, together with various minor inaccuracies, he had set the career of Bâbu-aḫ-iddina some fifty years too early.[3] Ebeling, in a later treatment of several of the texts,[4] did not advance beyond Koschaker, but accepted, at least as a possibility, the dating of Aššur-aḫ-iddina perhaps a century before his time.[5] Schroeder's article on the Boğazkoy *lîmu*-list[6] and Weidner, in his own thorough study,[7] offered valuable material and conclusions. But each covered only a restricted segment of the material and, therefore, inevitably advanced hypotheses which could not be maintained. In his own investigation, for example, Weidner saw no difficulty in dating a tablet of Iddin-Kubi, who flourished in the reigns of Erîba-Adad and Aššur-uballiṭ, as "probably" belonging to the reign of Tukulti-Ninurta.[8]

Thus, in evaluating Weidner's conclusions, the first requisite is a new examination of the chronological sequence of the legal and business documents of the Middle-Assyrian period. The first part of these studies attempts such an investigation. Free use has been made of the various published transliterations and translations of a number of the tablets. In particular, Ebeling's collection of the proper names[9] has been of especial usefulness, even though there was need, on many occasions, to take issue with his conclusions. Above all, thanks are due to Professor Julius Lewy, who introduced me to the reading of these texts, and whose helpful suggestions have guided every phase of this investigation.

[2] *NRU*, pp 6 ff

[3] *Ibid*, p 8, note 1

[4] Ebeling, E, *Urkunden des Archivs von Assur* (*MAOG*, VII, parts 1 & 2, hereafter abbreviated *Urkunden*), pp 57 ff

[5] *Ibid*, p 85, s v *KAJ* 100

[6] *AK*, I, pp 88 f

[7] *Op cit*

[8] *Ibid*, on *KAJ* 165, p 118

[9] *Eigennamen*.

CHAPTER I

The Fifteenth Century

I. The Middle-Assyrian Juridical and Business Documents published by Ebeling[1] were produced over the course of some three hundred years from the fifteenth to the twelfth centuries B. C.[2] Only in a few instances can any tablet be dated with precision. Nevertheless, more than three quarters of the material can be classified into four groups, each group consisting of roughly contemporary tablets;[3] and even within these groups, some kind of chronological sequence can frequently be determined.

Eight of the documents come from the earliest of these periods, the reigns of Aššur-nirâri II and Aššur-bêl-nišêšu (1423–1408),[4] and are considered in this chapter. In the succeeding chapters, the dating of the later tablets will similarly be determined. Finally, on the basis of this chronology, some remarks will be made on the development of Assyrian religion and culture during the centuries which are illustrated by our sources.

II. The following documents, by mentioning the name of the contemporary king, can be dated accurately:

1. *KAJ* 177 (Aššur-nirâri [II], line 10). Since the grandson of King Aššur-rabi is involved in the transaction (lines 7 f), the

[1] *KAJ*

[2] Ebeling gives 1500–1130 as the minimum range of dates (*Eigennamen*) However, five tablets of the collection are to be excluded as being of Neo- or Late Assyrian origin (140, 196, 270, 285, 287 Cf Weidner, *AfO*, XIII, p 317)

[3] The groups into which the tablets may be divided are

1. The reigns of Aššur-nirâri II and Aššur-bêl-nišêšu (1423–1408),
2. The reigns of Erîba-Adad, Aššur-uballit, and Enlil-nirâri (1389–1317),
3. From the reign of Adad-nirâri I to the reign of Tukulti-Ninurta (1304–1206);
4. The rule of Ninurta-tukulti-Aššur (1133)

[4] On the dating of the Assyrian kings, see Poebel, *JNES*, II, pp 85 ff Weidner's dates for this period show a difference of one year (*AfO*, XIV, p. 368)

king mentioned in line 10 is undoubtedly Aššur-nirâri II, the immediate successor of Aššur-rabi I.[5]

2. *KAJ* 162 (Aššur-bêl-nišêšu, lines 2, 8).

3. *KAJ* 172 (Aššur-bêl-nišêšu, line 3).[6]

4. *KAJ* 174 (Belonging to the reign either of Aššur-nirâri or of Aššur-bêl-nišêšu). The *lîmu* of this tablet is given as *Ber-nâdin-aḫḫê mâr Aššur-nirâri uklim* (lines 10 f.) Conceivably, Ber-nâdin-aḫḫê might have been appointed as *lîmu*-officer after the death of his father, and thus the date of the tablet is not to be more accurately determined.[7]

On the basis of *KAJ* 174, the following tablets are to be set

[5] Cf Koschaker, *NRU*, p 6

[6] Cf *Urkunden*, p 87 On items 2 and 3, cf Koschaker, *op cit*, p 7

[7] Ebeling's dating of the tablet in the reign of Aššur-nirâri III (*Urkunden*, p 78) undoubtedly does not intend to place this document in the thirteenth century, but rather has reference to an earlier chronology of Weidner (*Studien zur Chron*, pp 37 f), where an additional Aššur-nirâri is introduced, whose reign is set in the twentieth century In his *Konige von Assyrien*, however, Weidner points out that the first two Aššur-nirâri's of his earlier classification are actually the same person (Aššur-nirâri I), whose reign he then placed in the sixteenth century (The Khorsabad King List, however, shows that the first years of the fifteenth century is the correct date Cf Poebel, *loc cit*, etc) Hence it was recognized even before the publication of the Khorsabad King List that the king referred to in the *Studien* as Aššur-nirâri III should actually be known as Aššur-nirâri II

Although Ebeling elsewhere uses Weidner's later chronology, it is evident that the monarch referred to in our document belongs to the fifteenth century, and not to the reign of Aššur-nirâri III (1202–1197) The *lîmu*, Ber-nâdin-aḫḫê, mentioned here as the son of the king, is, as Ebeling has pointed out (*Eigennamen*, p 34), the grandfather of the witness in *KAJ* 8, where his name appears in the sequence·

(line 25) ^{d}*Šamaš-ki-di-nu mâr Ibašši-ilu mâr* ^{d}*Be-ir na-din-a-ḫi uklim*

Since, as will be shown, *KAJ* 8 belongs to the reign of Aššur-uballit, the father of Ber-nâdin-aḫḫê mentioned in *KAJ* 174 can be only Aššur-nirâri II This conclusion is confirmed by a reference to *KAJ* 64, a tablet which belongs to the reign of Erîba-Adad, and which mentions as creditor the same Ibašši-ilu, son of Ber-nâdin-aḫḫê, who appears in *KAJ* 8 as the father of the witness The identity and date of this Ber-nâdin-aḫḫê, as well as a reference to his son in a votive bead found at Tanis, is fully discussed by Julius Lewy, "The Middle Assyrian Votive Bead Found at Tanis," *Ignace Goldziher Memorial Volume*, I, pp 326 f

in the general period of the reigns of Aššur-nirâri and Aššur-bêl-nišêšu:

5. *KAJ* 139; 132. That these tablets are contemporary with *KAJ* 174 is shown by the following considerations·

a) *KAJ* 139 deals with four persons, whose names are given, without patronymic, as Dugul-ili (lines 3, 20), Abu-ṭâb (lines 5, 15, 18), Ibašši-ilu (lines 7, 13, 19), and Eriš-Kubi (lines 17, 20) [8]

b) The four men are shown to be brothers.

i) The first two persons mentioned in *KAJ* 139, Dugul-ili and Abu-ṭâb, appear in *KAJ* 132, 4 f. as the sons of Mâr-Šamaš

ii) An *Ibašši-ilu mâr Mâr-Šamaš* is known from *KAJ* 174, 9.

c) That Mâr-Šamaš, the father mentioned in *KAJ* 132, is the same person as the father mentioned in *KAJ* 174 is shown by the following considerations:

i) The transaction recorded in *KAJ* 132 consists of the sale of land in the district of ^{al}*Ṣu-ba-ti* (line 3) by the brothers Abu-ṭâb and Dugul-ili. *KAJ* 174 tells of the transfer by Ibašši-ilu of property which is likewise in ^{al}*Ṣu-ba-ti* and its district (line 6)

ii) The two documents were written by the same scribe, Šumu-libši (*KAJ* 132, 25; 174, rev 7).[9]

Clearly, therefore, *KAJ* 132 and 139 are contemporary

[8] That there are no more than the four persons dealt with in the references quoted is shown by lines 18–20

[pa-ḫ]a-at ^{m}*A-bu-tâb za-ak-ku-e* (line 19) [^{m}*Ib*]*ašši-ilu-ma it-ta-na-aš-ši* (line 20) [^{m}*Eriš*] *-Ku-bi ù* ^{m}*Du-gul-ili za-ku-ú*

If, for example, more than one Ibašši-ilu were involved in lines 7 and 13, it would be necessary for the document to state which of the two is intended in line 19 Thus the *KI MIN* (="ditto") following these names in the documents does not function as a restrictive (e g toponymic) attribute to distinguish the four men from others of the same name

[9] It becomes apparent, therefore, why the patronymic is omitted throughout *KAJ* 139 Evidently the missing opening lines of the tablet must have spoken of the *mârê*^{meš} ^{m}*Mâr-Šamaš*

with *KAJ* 174, and are to be set in the period of the reigns of Aššur-nirâri and Aššur-bêl-nišêšu [10]

The following documents are close contemporaries of *KAJ* 162, which we have assigned to the reign of Aššur-bêl-nišêšu:

6. *KAJ* 22; 50 The following persons occur in two or more of the three tablets, *KAJ* 22; 50; and 162.

a) *Urad-Šerua mâr Aššur-iqîša* is mentioned in all three of the documents either as the creditor or the receiver of a pledge (*KAJ* 22, 5; 50, 3; 162, 14 f.);

b) *Ilu-tišmar mâr Apuḫija*, the depositor of the pledge in *KAJ* 162 (lines 18 f.), is a witness to the transaction in *KAJ* 50 (line 20);

c) His brother, *Išme-Adad mâr Apuḫija*, is the debtor of *KAJ* 22 (line 6) and *KAJ* 50 (line 4);

d) The scribe of *KAJ* 22, *Mâr-Idigla mâr Kubi-eriš*, is likewise a witness in *KAJ* 50 (*KAJ* 22, 21; 50, 21).

The recurrence of a single figure might allow for a difference in decades in the time of origin of the documents; but when

[10] It is doubtful whether the *lîmu* of *KAJ* 132, 28

() is to be identified with the *lîmu*

of *KAJ* 37, 23 (. Cf. Ebeling, *Eigennamen*, p. 91). One suspects that the *lîmu* of *KAJ* 37 is possibly to be identified with the *lîmu* of *KAJ* 85, a contemporary document, line 30 of which is to be read: *li-mu* ^{m}*Ṭâb-*^{d}*Ištar* ().

Note, at any rate, the strange writing of *A-šur* in *KAJ* 37, 23 It should also be pointed out that there is considerable space to the left of the *lîmu* as it stands in *KAJ* 132. This, together with the unusual spelling of *ṭâb* makes one suspect the restoration of the name, although if *tâb* can be written once as

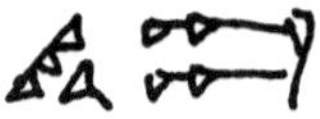 (*ṭâb*^{ab}), then the possibility of a writing  (*ṭâb*^{áb}) should not be excluded.

creditor, debtor, and witnesses correspond, the documents in question may, without danger, be considered roughly contemporary.

The above tablets and their eponymies are listed in Table I, and constitute the entire group which may at present be assigned to the fifteenth century.

TABLE I

DOCUMENTS AND EPONYMIES OF THE FIFTEENTH CENTURY

1. Reign of Aššur-nirâri

TABLET NO.	Lîmu
KAJ 177	Aššur-mutakkıl mâr Adad-eriš

2. Reign of Aššur-nirâri *or* Aššur-bêl-nišêšu

KAJ 132	Ṭâb-Aššur (?)
KAJ 174	Ber-nâdın-aḫḫê mâr Aššur-nırârı uklım
KAJ 139	Unstated

3. Reign of Aššur-bêl-nišêšu

KAJ 22	Bêl-qarrâd mâr Aššur-rabı
KAJ 162	Šamaš-kıdınnu mâr Adad-da'ıq
KAJ 172	Manu-bal-Aššur
KAJ 50	Unstated

CHAPTER II

The Fourteenth Century

The more numerous tablets which have been preserved from the succeeding centuries present a fuller picture of the economic life of Aššur in the Middle-Assyrian period, and in particular of the transactions of several families of money lenders and administrative officials. In the fourteenth century, a certain Bêl-qarrâd and the families of Nûr-Kubi and Iddin-Kubi are the most frequently attested in their capacity as money lenders. The transactions of these families are discussed after a chronological introduction to the period as a whole.

Part 1. General Chronology

I. The following documents may be directly assigned to the reign of Erîba-Adad:[1]

1. *KAJ* 160 (see line 8. Cf. Ebeling, *Urkunden*, page 77).

2. *KAJ* 183 (and *KAV* 93) (see line 4. Cf. Ebeling, *Urkunden*, p. 89).

3. *KAJ* 20. The *lîmu, Aššur-lî mâr Ibašši-ilu mâr Šuzub-ili* occurs also in the dating of *KAJ* 183, where he is mentioned without his patronymic merely as *Aššur-lî*. There is little doubt concerning the identification of the eponymy years of these two documents, since·

   a) *KAJ* 20 is contemporary with *KAJ* 14 (*Šamaš-râm-kittum mâr Šamaš-tukulti* is the scribe of both tablets); and

   b) *KAJ* 14, being a tablet of Iddin-Kubi belongs approximately in the reign of Erîba-Adad, as is shown below.

[1] 1389–1363 It is evident that this is the king referred to in our documents, since two of the great merchants mentioned in these transactions, *Iddin-Kubi mâr Rîš-Nabû* and his son, *Kidin-Adad*, were active partly in the reign of an Erîba-Adad and partly in the reign of an Aššur-uballiṭ. Since Aššur-uballiṭ I was the immediate successor of Erîba-Adad (1362–1327), the identification is beyond doubt

4. *KAV* 209 (affixed with the seal of Erība-Adad, as is noted in Schroeder's introduction, *KAV*, page XI)

5. *KAJ* 64.[2] The *līmu* of this document (line 26), read by Ebeling as *Aššur-bêl-*[*apli*?], is to be read *Aššur-bêl-k*[*a-la*] in accordance with the *līmu* of *KAV* 209 (line 9).[3]

6. *KAJ* 147. This tablet deals with the sale by Apuḫija, the son of Labunija, of a piece of land in the region of Gubbi-êkallim (line 5) The purchaser is Admati-ılu, the son of Aššur-lî. In all probability Apuḫija is the son of the same Labunija whose grandson borrowed lead from Iddın-Kubi on the security of land, likewise in the region of Gubbı-êkallım (*KAJ* 14, 10).

Moreover, Labunija, the grandfather of the debtor in *KAJ* 14, seems likewise to be found in *KAJ* 61; 161; and 163, since in these documents, also, his descendants become indebted to the family of Iddin-Kubi. In *KAJ* 61, it is recorded that Asiru, the grandson of Labunija, borrowed grain from Kidın-Adad. By means of *KAJ* 161, Kıdin-Adad acquired an earlier tablet of the indebtedness of the sons of Labunija, which was transferred to him by a former creditor, Qîš-Amurru. Finally by means of *KAJ* 163, an earlier debt sustained by the grandsons of Labunija to *Şıllı-Kubı mâr Iqıšeja* is transferred by the sons of Şilli-Kubi, once again to Kidın-Adad.[4] These tablets reveal part of a systematic attempt of Kıdin-Adad to obtain possession of the debts, and ultimately, no doubt, of the property of the descendants of Labunija.[5]

On the basis of these identifications, the genealogy of

---

[2] Republished in the same work (*KAJ*) as No 68

[3] Thus Ungnad, *RLA*, p 442; likewise Weıdner, *AfO*, XIII, p 312, on the basis of an inspection of the original

[4] *KAJ* 23 mentions another grandson of the same Labunıja, although Labunıja is not here mentioned by name Ilušu-nammır, son of Šıme-nada, who in this tablet borrows lead from *Şıllı-Kubı mâr Iqıšêja*, is the brother of the two sons of *Šıme-nada mâr Labunıja* who likewise had borrowed from Şıllı-Kubı as a preliminary to the transaction of *KAJ* 163 (Cf *KAJ* 64, which mentions the three brothers by name as the sons of Šıme-nada)

[5] Note also *KAJ* 12, a tablet of indebtedness of Sınıja and Amur-dannûssa, grandsons of Labunıja, to Iddın-Kubı, and *KAJ* 29, a tablet of the indebtedness of Asırıja, likewise a grandson of Labunıja, to the same creditor

TABLE II.

THE GENEALOGY OF LABUNIẠA

Aššur-qarrâd
- (*KAJ* 147) ↓ Labuniịa
  - (*KAJ* 14) ↓ Sîn-nâdin-aḫḫê ↓ Ibašši-ilu
  - (*KAJ* 61) (cf. *KAJ* 29) ↓ Az[uniịa] ↓ Asiru (=Asiriịa, *KAJ* 29)
  - (*KAJ* 147) ↓ Apuḫiịa
  - (*KAJ* 161) ↓ Aššur-nâdin-aḫı (and brothers)
  - (*KAJ* 163) ↓ Šime-nada
    - (cf. *KAJ* 64)
      - (*KAJ* 23) ↓ Ilušu-nammir
      - (*KAJ* 163)
        - ↓ Iqišeịa
          - (*KAJ* 12) ↓ Amur-dannûssa
        - ↓ Sîni

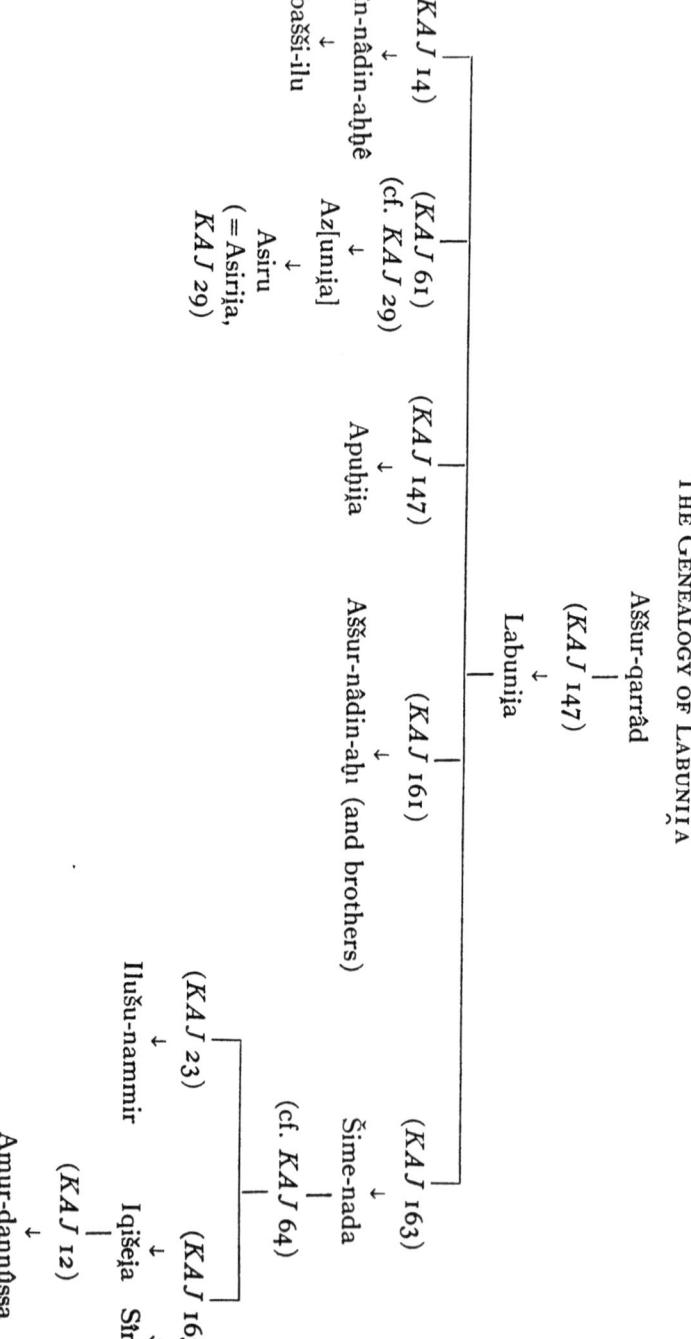

Labunija, as given in Table II, may be established It follows, from the same identifications, that *KAJ* 147 is a document parallel to those preliminary documents which are disposed of in *KAJ* 161 and 163; it is probably closer in time to the tablet mentioned in *KAJ* 161, which dealt with a debt of the sons rather than of the grandsons of Labunija.

Apparently, therefore, the tablet belongs to a time before the activity of Iddin-Kubi, or at least before the time of Kidin-Adad, both of whom flourished in the reigns of Erîba-Adad and Aššur-uballit, as will be shown below. It cannot be later, therefore, than the reign of Erîba-Adad. This method for dating *KAJ* 147 is outlined by Ebeling (*Urkunden*, p. 67), who reaches a similar conclusion.

The succeeding documents mention by name some of the persons who are known, from the above tablets, to have lived in the reign of Erîba-Adad. It is possible, of course, that considerable time may have elapsed between the preparation of the various documents in which they participated. For this reason they are assigned, only approximately, to the reign of Erîba-Adad.

7. *KAJ* 1. Note the following parallel with *KAJ* 147
KAJ 147, 26:
maḫar Ú-[ṣur]-ki-nu mâr Uš-šur-a-na-^{d}Marduk
KAJ 1, lines 29 f.:
maḫar Ú-ṣur-ki-nu mâr Uš-šur-a-na-[^{d}Marduk]

8. *KAJ* 52; 176 These documents were produced by the same scribe (*Iddin-Marduk mâr Apil-Kubi*) as *KAJ* 1, and are therefore roughly contemporary.

9 *KAJ* 25 This document (line 24) appears to have the same *lîmu*, Iâkku-limmir, as *KAJ* 52 (line 28).

It is not impossible, however, that the documents discussed under items 7, 8, and 9 are to be placed in the reign of Aššur-uballiṭ. In the first place, the debtor of *KAJ* 25, *Bêl-mušallim mâr Šamaš-uballiṭ* (line 5) may appear as witness to *KAJ* 151 (lines 24 f.); 153 (lines 24, 30); and 155 (lines 25, 31).[6] The

[6] See below, pp 205 ff , for the dating of these tablets

father's name has not been fully preserved in these tablets, but appears as follows:

KAJ 151, 25:

KAJ 153, 24.

KAJ 155, 25.

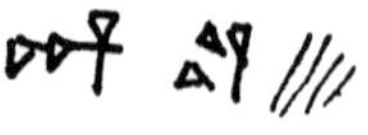

The three tablets are contemporary, and without doubt have reference to the same witness; and while the traces of *KAJ* 153 might suggest the name ^{d}Šamaš-da[mmıq], the traces of *KAJ* 151 would be in perfect accord with the name Šamaš-uballıṭ.

In addition, *KAJ* 154, a further contemporary of *KAJ* 151; 153; and 155, has at least one participant in common with *KAJ* 1 [7] For this reason it is perhaps best to set these tablets in the last years of Erîba-Adad, with the concession that the first years of Aššur-uballıṭ are not to be excluded.

10. *KAJ* 14; 148 (cf. Ebeling, *Urkunden*, p. 63).

a) The scribe of *KAJ* 14 (lines 23 f.) is given as Šamaš-râm-kıttum mâr Šamaš-tukultı; the same scribe appears in *KAJ* 20 (lines 23 f) Note, also, that Mâr-Šerua, the son of Aššur-qarrâd, is a witness to *KAJ* 14 (lıne 20) and lıkewıse to *KAJ* 64 (lıne 19). In *KAJ* 14, his name is wrıtten.
maḫar Mâr-[^{d}Š]e-ru-a mâr ^{d}[A-šur]-qarrâd
In *KAJ* 64, we read
maḫar Mâr-^{d}Š[e-ru-a mâr] ^{d}A-[šur]-qarrâd.
On thıs basis, it appears safe to assign the tablet to the reign of Erîba-Adad.

b) The *lîmu* of *KAJ* 148 (lınes 39 f.) is the same as that of *KAJ* 14 (lines 27 f.), namely Aššur-mušêzıb mâr Kıdın-Enlıl.

11. *KAJ* 179. Thıs tablet ıs to be dated on the basıs of *KAJ* 14. In both documents, (179, 26; 14, 21), Mâr-Šerua mâr Abusı appears as witness (cf. *Urkunden*, p 86. On *KAJ* 179, compare also p 222 and note 44, below

---

[7] See below, p 210, for a full dıscussıon of this point

II. The following documents may be directly assigned to the reign of Aššur-uballiṭ:

1. *KAJ* 173 (=*KAV* 210). (See line 5. Cf. Ebeling, *Urkunden*, p. 88.)

2. *KAJ* 36, written in the eponymy of the same *lîmu*, Adad-nâsir, as *KAJ* 173.

3. *KAJ* 18; 27; 60; 99. The eponymy of Enlil-mudammiq is given in *KAH* II, 27, 31, which is a building inscription of the reign of Aššur-uballiṭ I (cf. *AOB*, I, p. 42). The above documents are assigned to the reign of this king on the basis of the same eponymy (thus, *KAJ* 18, 26; 27, 28; 60, 26; 99, 30).

4. *KAV* 211 (see line 2).

5. *KAJ* 13; 161. These tablets have the same eponymy, that of Adad-mušêzib, as *KAV* 211 (cf. Ebeling, *Urkunden*, p. 78). The recurrence of *Kidin-Adad mâr Iddin-Kubi* in *KAV* 211; *KAJ* 13; and *KAJ* 161 proves that the *lîmu* given in *KAJ* 13 and 161 as *Adad-mušêzib mâr Šuzub-Marduk* is the same as that given in *KAV* 211 merely as *Adad-mušêzib*, without the patronymic.

A fragment of a *lîmu*-list[8] discovered at Boğazköy (*KUB* IV, 93) demonstrates that this eponymy followed immediately upon that of Enlil-mudammiq, given in rubric 3, above.

6. *KAJ* 170 (cf. Ebeling, *Urkunden*, p. 84). This is an undated tablet which has reference to the same transaction as is

[8] The list, in Schroeder's transliteration (*AK*, I, 88), is as follows:

2 [^{d}]a-šur-mu(?)-[ ]
3 [^{d}]en-lil-^{mu}mudammiq
4 [^{d}]adad-^{mu}mušêzib
5 ^{d}a-šur-šum-usur
6 ^{d}a-šur-nâdin-šum[âti^{meš}]
7 ni-ik-an[u] (to be read Ibašši-ilu A full account of the relevant literature is given by Lewy, "Tanis Bead," p 317)
8 li-bur-[za-nin]
9 ni-[ ]

The succession of two known *lîmu*'s from the reign of Aššur-uballit as items 3 and 4 of this list make it clear that the fragment has been correctly interpreted as a *lîmu*-list from this reign See further on *KAJ* 17, below.

undertaken in *KAV* 211. *KAJ* 170 refers to the sale of a female carpenter by Ibašši-ilu and Sarniqu, the sons of Šamaš-sime; the purchaser is *Kidin-Adad mâr Iddin-Kubi*. *KAV* 211, a slightly later document, acknowledges the possession by Kidin-Adad of the children of this bondmaid. The witnessing of this tablet by *Adad-pilaḫ mâr Mâr-Idigla* (170, 25), who is also a witness to *KAJ* 99 (line 23), confirms this dating of *KAJ* 170 as perhaps a year or so earlier than *KAV* 211.[9]

7. *KAJ* 17;[10] 19, 164[11] The *lîmu* of these documents, Aššur-šum-uṣur, immediately follows the *lîmu* of *KAJ* 13; 161; and

[9] It is surprising that Ebeling does not identify the Ibašši-ilu of *KAV* 211, 7, rev 5, with the Ibašši-ilu of *KAJ* 170 (*Eigennamen*, p 43) Note also the traces of "*ù* ^{m}[*Sa*]-*ar*-[*ni-qu*]" in line 8 of *KAV* 211

[10] A further indication of the date of *KAJ* 17 may be seen in its relationship to *KAV* 209 *KAV* 209, one of the several documents of indebtedness to *Bêl-qarrâd mâr Urad-Kubi*, stems from the reign of Erîba-Adad (see p 195, above) *KAJ* 17 acknowledges a debt of the son of the same Bêl-qarrâd to *Kidin-Adad mâr Iddin-Kubi* The debt may, of course, have been contracted during the lifetime of the debtor's father, or it may be somewhat later But at any rate, the transaction makes the reign of Aššur-uballit the most likely period for the origin of this contract

[11] A comparison of *KAJ* 164 with *KAJ* 172, a document of the reign of Aššur-bêl-nišêšu (see above, page 190), gives additional confirmation of this chronology *KAJ* 164 is one of a series of three tablets (*KAJ* 164, 172, and 175) which describe the ultimate transfer of the property of *Bur-šarru mâr Bêliia* to a certain Aḫu-tâb and his son, Naḫiš-šalme

On the basis of these three tablets, the genealogy of the family of Bur-šarru may be reconstructed as follows

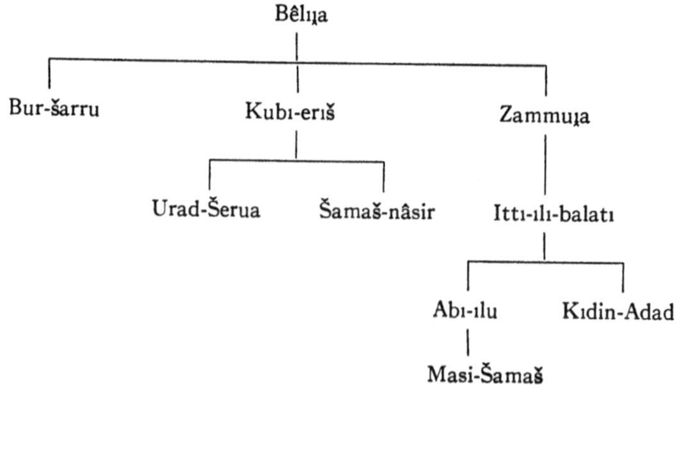

KAV 211, in the *lîmu*-list *KUB* IV, 93. Since the scribe of *KAJ* 17, Enlil-mudammiq mâr Abu-ṭâb (line 20), is the scribe, likewise, of *KAJ* 170 (line 27), we have additional evidence that *KUB* IV, 93 has been correctly interpreted as a *lîmu*-list.

8. *Either* a) *KAJ* 26; *KAJ* 149; and *KAJ* 152
Or b) *KAJ* 12; *KAJ* 63.

The eponymy year of Ibašši-ilu, which is seventh in the *lîmu*-list *KUB* IV, 93, cannot be identified with certainty. It may be identified with the eponymy of the tablets of group a), the *lîmu* of which is given as *Ibašši-ilu mâr Aššur-bêl-apli* (*KAJ* 26, 27 f.;[12] 149, 34 f.; 152, 30 f.). Since *KAJ* 26

Apparently, Bur-šarru died without children, and as a result, part of his property fell to the crown, and part went to at least one of his brothers, Kubi-eriš, and his children The property of Kubi-eriš and his sons was purchased by Zammuia and his son, as a preliminary to our transactions, which took place as follows·

i) *KAJ* 172 This treats of the crown's portion of his property, which had been given to a certain Eriš-Kubi By means of this tablet, Eriš-Kubi transfers the land to Aḫu-tâb

ii) *KAJ* 175 deals with the share of one of the brothers, Kubi-eriš, which he had sold to another brother, Zammuia By means of this tablet, the grandsons of Zammuia, Abi-ilu and Kidin-Adad, transfer the property to Naḫiš-šalme, the son of Aḫu-tâb Presumably, the Aḫu-tâb intended is none other than the purchaser in *KAJ* 172

iii) *KAJ* 164 deals with the share of the sons of Kubi-eriš, which had originally been treated in a similar way, falling into the possession of the son of Zammuia, Itti-ili-balati In this tablet, the land is transferred by Masi-Šamaš, the grandson of Itti-ili-balati, to the same Naḫiš-šalme as had acquired the land of Kubi-eriš in *KAJ* 175

On the basis of this sequence, it is clear that *KAJ* 172 is at least one generation older than *KAJ* 175, and at least two generations older than *KAJ* 164 *KAJ* 175 and *KAJ* 164 may, of course, be contemporary, or there may be a generation difference between them At any rate, since *KAJ* 172 belongs to the reign of Aššur-bêl-nišêšu, the remaining documents may well be assigned to the reign of Aššur-uballit

[12] Reading in *KAJ* 26, with Ebeling (cf *Eigennamen*, p 43)·
(line 27) *li-mu* ᵐ*Ibašši-ilu*
(line 28) *mâr* [*A-šur-bêl*]-*apli*

The *lîmu* of *KAJ* 142, given merely as *Ibašši-ilu*, without patronymic, is probably to be identified with one of these two officers; and since the father's name is not given, the earlier of the two would appear the most likely. But

is a tablet of *Iddin-Kubi mâr Rîš-Nabû* and *KAJ* 149 is a document of *Kidin-Adad* (on whose dates, see below, pp. 222 f), the eponymy, in any case, belongs in this general period.

On the other hand, *Ibašši-ilu mâr Niruabi* (*KAJ* 12, 29 f.; 63, 28) is just as likely to be the *lîmu*-officer in question. *KAJ* 12, which was written in his eponymy, is, like *KAJ* 26, an Iddin-Kubi tablet; *KAJ* 63, written in the same year, is, like *KAJ* 149, a Kidin-Adad tablet. Thus, we have no satisfactory means of choosing between these two possibilities.[13]

9 Regarding the identification of *KUB* IV, 93, line 8.

Schroeder[14] tentatively suggests the identification of the eighth name of this *lîmu*-list with the *lîmu* known from four of our documents as Libur-zânin-Aššur (*KAJ* 88, 29; 168, 28; 218, 11; 318, 15) Nevertheless, the alternate suggestion of Weidner must be accepted, which identifies the *lîmu* of these four tablets with the man who is mentioned in *KAJ* 116, rev. 6, and likewise in *Assur* 9819, line 12[15] *KAJ* 116 is undoubtedly from the general period of Shalmaneser/Tukulti-Ninurta; and the restoration of line rev. 3

[Li-bur]-za-nin-^{d}[A-šur ša] rêš (šarri)

which of the two is earlier cannot be determined On the approximate dating of *KAJ* 142 in the reign of Aššur-uballit, see below, p 208

It should be pointed out, however, that the tablet cannot be dated on the basis of the name "*Erimkîni*" It is by no means certain that the Erim-kîni who is the debtor of *KAJ* 142 (lines 4 f) is likewise the grandfather of one of the witnesses of *KAJ* 20 (Cf Ebeling, *Eigennamen*, p 40) To be sure, since *KAJ* 20 belongs in the reign of Erîba-Adad, the identification, which would make *KAJ* 142 some years later, is not impossible But the recurrence of a single name in this way cannot be considered conclusive

As regards *KAJ* 82, where the *lîmu* is given (line 10) as *[Ib]ašši-ilu tupšarru*, we have no evidence for dating the tablet, nor for the identification of this *lîmu* with any of the above

[13] Cf Schroeder, *loc cit*, who also does not preclude the possibility that the *lîmu* of *KAJ* 82 may be the Ibašši-ilu in question (see the final paragraph of note 16) But since, in any event, the other two eponymy years are to be dated in the reign of Aššur-uballiṭ, the choice of the eponymy of *KAJ* 82 for this position does not appear probable

[14] *Loc cit*

[15] *AfO*, XIII, p 115

(cf. *KAJ* 218, 2 f.; 318, 2 f.) shows that this tablet is dealing with the *lîmu*-officer of the other four contracts Thus, *KUB* IV, 93, 8 is not to be reconstructed on the basis of the documents in *KAJ* which belong to a considerably later period than the *lîmu*-list.

10. *KAV* 212 (see line 6).

11. *KAJ* 6. This document appears to have the same *lîmu*, *Aššur-kîna-idi mâr Šuzub-Marduk* (lines 36 f) as *KAV* 212, the *lîmu* of which (line 14) is given simply as *Aššur-kîna-idi*. Additional evidence that *KAJ* 6 belongs to this period, and that these two eponymy years are to be identified is to be found in the following consideration. A certain *Iâkku-limmir mâr Uššur-ana-(Marduk!)* appears as a witness to *KAJ* 6 (lines 27 f.). Evidently the same person is intended in *KAJ* 36, where line 4 is to be read:

[^{m}*Ia-a-ku-li-me*]-*ir mâr Uš-šur-a-na-*^{d}*Marduk*.[16]

Since *KAJ* 36 likewise belongs to the reign of Aššur-uballiṭ, it is reasonable to identify the eponymy years of *KAJ* 6 and of *KAV* 212.

12. *KAJ* 8. The *lîmu* of this tablet is Abu-ṭâb, the son of King Erîba-Adad. Thus *KAJ* 8 must have been drawn up during the reign of Erîba-Adad or shortly thereafter. Since Aššur-uballiṭ ruled for thirty-six years,[17] his reign is the latest likely date for this document.

On the other hand, the relationship between *KAJ* 8 and *KAJ* 10 makes the earlier dating of *KAJ* 8 in the reign of Erîba-Adad equally unlikely *KAJ* 8 deals with the method by which a part of the property of Amurru-nâṣir is to be divided among his sons. Amurru-nâṣir agrees that a *sikiltum*[18] be-

16 The possibility of this reading is given by Ebeling (*Eigennamen*, p 93) under the heading Uššur-ana-Marduk, although it is ignored under the heading Iâkku-limmir (*Ibid*, page 42) Ebeling was unable to date the document with certainty (*Urkunden*, p 82)

17 Thus the Khorsabad King List, rev I, lines 13 f, transliterated by Weidner, *AfO*, XIV, page 363

18 J Lewy has suggested "acquisition" as a suitable translation for *sikiltum* This derivation from the root *sakâlu*, as he interprets it in *CH*, VIIr, 39 f ("If a married woman [lines 39 f.] intends to make an acquisi-

longing to one of his sons, Parparaịau, shall not be claimed by his other sons. In *KAJ* 10, the division among the sons has already been made and is accepted by Parparaịau.

However, *KAJ* 10 belongs, as will be shown, in the reign of Adad-nirâri I (see below, p. 235) and is thus considerably later than *KAJ* 8. It is clear, therefore, that time elapsed between the writing of the two documents, and probably Amurru-nâṣir had died in the meanwhile. But if *KAJ* 8 is set back into the reign of Erîba-Adad, it would mean that over fifty-eight years had passed between the writing of the two documents,[19] and such an eventuality is clearly unlikely.

13. *KAJ* 11. The following parallels occur between *KAJ* 60 and *KAJ* 11

a) The creditor in both cases is *Iddin-Kubi mâr Rîš-Nabû* (*KAJ* 11, 4; 60, 4).

b) The scribe in both cases is *Daịịânu mâr Adad-šamši* (*KAJ* 11, 23; 60, 23 f.).

c) A further witness is common to both tablets, viz., *Puḫunu mâr Urad-Tašmeti* (*KAJ* 11, 20; 60, 21).

d) The son of the remaining witness of *KAJ* 60 (line 20, *Ili-mâlik mâr Iddin-bêl*) is, presumably, the remaining witness of *KAJ* 11 (line 21, *Šamaš-uballiṭ mâr Ili-mâlik*). This is a natural substitution, since Ili-mâlik is the debtor of *KAJ* 11 (lines 5 f.), and could not have witnessed his own transaction.

Since there are so many parallels between these two documents, it is safe to assume that they were written in close succession to one another, and that *KAJ* 11 is to be dated, on the basis of *KAJ* 60, in the reign of Aššur-uballiṭ.

The succeeding documents mention by name some of the persons who are known, from the above tablets, to have lived

tion," i e "spend money") would give a very acceptable sense in this document

[19] The total of the years given for the reigns of Aššur-uballit (36), Enlil-nirâri (10) and Arik-dên-ili (12), according to the Khorsabad King List (Poebel, *JNES*, II, p 87, Weidner, *AfO*, XIV, p 368)

in the reign of Aššur-uballiṭ. Once again, however, since considerable time may have elapsed between the preparation of the various documents in which they participated, we should assign them only approximately to the reign of this king.

A. Based on parallels with *KAJ* 60 (and *KAJ* 11).

14. *KAJ* 29. *Daiiânu mâr Adad-šamši*, the scribe of *KAJ* 29 (line 22), is likewise the scribe of *KAJ* 11 (line 23) and *KAJ* 60 (lines 23 f). On the other hand, a parallel with *KAJ* 64 might make the last years of Erîba-Adad a possible date for this tablet; note that *Sinniia mâr Šime-nada*, one of the debtors of *KAJ* 64 (lines 4 ff.), is mentioned as a witness in *KAJ* 29 (line 20).

15. *KAJ* 86 *Puḫunu mâr Urad-Tašmetı* appears as witness in *KAJ* 86 (lines 13 f.) as well as in *KAJ* 60 (line 21) and *KAJ* 11 (line 20).

16. *KAJ* 67. *Ilı-mâlık mâr Iddın-Bêl*, a witness in *KAJ* 67, 22, appears likewise as witness in *KAJ* 60, 20, and is the debtor of *KAJ* 11, lines 5 f. There is no doubt, therefore, that the *līmu* of this tablet (line 27) is to be read, in accordance with *KAJ* 86, line 19:

lı-mu Ṣi-na-a.

17. *KAJ* 53; 153; and 155.[20]

a) Ili-mâlık mâr Iddin-bêl (see the previous paragraph) is the debtor of *KAJ* 53 (line 5).

b) *KAJ* 153; and 155 were written in the same year as *KAJ* 53, the *līmu* of all documents being *Išme-Aššur mâr*

---

[20] Ebeling dates these tablets in the reign of Erîba-Adad, on the basis of the occurrence as scribe of *Bêl-aḫḫêšu mâr Amur-dannûssa*, who appears, likewise in *KAJ* 150, a tablet of Iddın-Kubı (*Urkunden*, pp 60 f)

However, we cannot maintain the conclusion of Koschaker (*NRU*, page 7, note 6) which Ebeling accepts, that Iddin-Kubi died during the reign of Erîba-Adad (see below, note 44) On the contrary, evidence of his activity in the reign of Aššur-uballıṭ is ample The conclusion of Ebeling is therefore highly questionable Furthermore, it is difficult to see why Ebeling, if he dates these tablets in the reign of Erîba-Adad, should nevertheless be willing to assign *KAJ* 150 to the reign of Aššur-uballıṭ (*op cıt*, page 72, see below on the dating of *KAJ* 150).

Erib-Aššur (*KAJ* 53, 29; 153, 28 f.; 155, 29 f. On the possibility of an earlier date, cf. pages 197 f., above).

Based on further parallels with *KAJ* 60.

18. *KAJ* 150; 151; 165; 229.

a) *Laqîpu mâr Ṣilli-Kubi* appears in *KAJ* 150 (line 12, cf. line 1) as the forfeiter of a pledge for lead borrowed from Iddin-Kubi. In *KAJ* 60, line 5, the same *Laqîpu mâr Ṣilli-Kubi* acknowledges a debt of grain from Iddin-Kubi.

b) *KAJ* 151; 165; and 229 were written in the same year as *KAJ* 150, the *lîmu*-year of these tablets appearing, respectively, as·

KAJ 151, 34 ^{md}*A-šur-i-din-na*
KAJ 165, 32 ^{md}*A-šur-i-din tupšarru*
KAJ 229, 8 ^{md}*A!-šur!-i-din*[21]
KAJ 150, 26 ^{md}*A-šur-i-din*.

That the same person is to be understood in these cases follows from these considerations:

i) *KAJ* 150, a contemporary of *KAJ* 60, belongs in the reign of Aššur-uballiṭ, as was shown above.

ii) *KAJ* 165 is a contemporary of *KAJ* 26. The debtor of *KAJ* 165 is *Kidin-Marduk mâr Aššur-qarrâd mâr Igaiae* (lines 7 f.); and the debtor of *KAJ* 26 is his brother, *Izqupiia mâr Aššur-qarrâd mâr Igaiae* (lines 6 f.). It will be shown below that *KAJ* 26 also belongs to the reign of Aššur-uballiṭ (page 207).

iii) *KAJ* 151 is contemporary to *KAJ* 153 and 155, likewise documents of this reign, as is shown above. *Bêl-mušallim mâr Šamaš-[uballiṭ]*, a witness to the transaction of *KAJ* 151 (line 25), is likewise a witness in *KAJ* 153, 24; and 155, 25[22]

Similarly, *KAJ* 151 is contemporary to *KAJ* 28, as can be shown on the basis of the creditor, *Kîniia mâr Nûr-Kubi* (*KAJ* 151, 11; 28, 5). It will be shown (see

[21] On the collation of Weidner, *AfO*, XIII, page 317, *s v* Šamaš-iddin

[22] The name is restored on the basis of the debtor of *KAJ* 25, 5

p. 209 below) that *KAJ* 28 also belongs to this period.[23]
iv) *KAJ* 229 is a document of Kidin-Adad, whose career, as will be shown, lay largely in the reign of Aššur-uballiṭ.

19. *KAJ* 152,[24] 26; and 149 (See item 8, above). *Laqîpu mâr Ṣilli-Kubi* is the debtor of *KAJ* 152, 7 and of *KAJ* 60, 5. Thus *KAJ* 152 comes from the reign of Aššur-uballiṭ

The *lîmu* of all three tablets is *Ibašši-ilu mâr Aššur-bêl-apli*. Further details concerning his eponymy will be found under item 8 above.

20. *KAJ* 96. The debtor of this tablet (line 4), as of *KAJ* 60, etc , is *Laqîpu mâr Ṣilli-Kubi*.

Based on parallels with rubrics 14–20, above

21 *KAJ* 12; 63. The *lîmu* of both of these tablets is given as *Ibašši-ilu mâr Niruabi* (*KAJ* 12, 29 f.; 63, 28; see rubric 8, above).

KAJ 12 may be dated on the following basis:

a) *Amur-dannûssa mâr Iqišeia* is one of the debtors of *KAJ* 12 (line 6) and one of the witnesses of *KAJ* 29 (line 19).

b) *Adad-kâbit mâr Pâliḫiia* is a witness in *KAJ* 12 (line 24) and in *KAJ* 53 (line 23).

c) *KAJ* 12 and *KAJ* 63 are close contemporaries of *KAJ* 26, as is seen in the following comparisons·

i) *KAJ* 63, 21 f. *maḫar Iz-ku-pi-ia mâr* [^{d}*A*]-*šur-qarrâd*.
KAJ 26, 6 *Iz-qu-pi-ia mâr* ^{d}*A-šur-qarrâd* (creditor).
KAJ 12, 23 *maḫar Iz-qu-pi-ia mâr* ^{d}*A-šur-qarrâd*.

ii) *KAJ* 63, 23 f. *maḫar* ^{d}*Amurru-mu-še-zi-ib tupšarru mâr* ^{d}*A-šur-*[*li*]*-bi-šu-nu*.
KAJ 26, 23 f. *maḫar* ^{d}*Amurru-mu-še-zi-ib tupšarrum*^{rum} *mâr* [^{d}*A-šur*]*-li-bi-šu-nu*.

[23] It should be noted that the eponymy of Aššur-iddin mentioned in *KAV* 135 belongs, as has been shown by J Lewy ("Das Alter der Listen *KAV* Nrr 135, 160, 167," *ZA*, XXXV, pages 43–46), to the Neo-Assyrian period, and is not to be identified with the eponymy of these documents

[24] On the basis of the scribe, Bêl-aḫḫêšu, Ebeling dates this tablet as well as *KAJ* 149, also, in the reign of Erîba-Adad (*op cit*, pp 64 f) See above, note 20, for a full evaluation of this criterion

22. *KAJ* 61 If the debtor, ^{m}*A-si-ru mâr A-z[u-ni-i̯a]* (line 4) is the same as ^{m}*A-si-ri-i̯a mâr A-zu-ni-i̯a* (*KAJ* 29, 5). Since *KAJ* 61 is a Kidin-Adad tablet, some support is given to this identification.

23. *KAJ* 157.[25] *Šamaš-pâṭir mâr Šamaš-nada* is the scribe of *KAJ* 157 (lines 12 f.), and a witness to *KAJ* 149 (line 27).

Based on rubrics 21–23.

24. *KAJ* 79 (=*KAJ* 166) This document has the following parallel to *KAJ* 12

KAJ 79, 6: *ù* ^{d}*Adad-kâbit mâr Pa-li-ḫi-i̯a* (a debtor)
KAJ 12, 24: *maḫar* ^{d}*Adad-kâbit mâr Pa-li-ḫi-i̯a.*[26]

25. *CT* 33, 15b. The *lîmu* of this tablet, Amurru-ma-ilu (line 14), is the same as that of *KAJ* 79 (line 28).

B. Additional documents, based on parallels with *KAJ* 27.

26. *KAJ* 175 The following parallel connects *KAJ* 175 with *KAJ* 27 and 164 (cf. Ebeling, *Urkunden*, p. 70).
KAJ 175, line 30: *a-na Na-ḫi-iš-šal-me mâr A-ḫu-ṭâbi*
KAJ 27, line 4: *ištu Na-ḫi-iš-šal-m[i mâr A]-ḫu-ṭâbi*
KAJ 164, lines 16 f.: *a-na* ^{m}*Na-ḫi-šal-mi mâr A-ḫu-ṭâbi*^{bi}.

27. *KAJ* 142[27] This document may be dated very roughly on the basis of *KAJ* 164; and 175. Note the following parallel:
KAJ 164, 9· *ugâr âli ša* ^{m}*I-di-ni*
KAJ 175, 3· *ugâr âli ša* ^{m}*I-din-ni*
KAJ 142, 11: *ugâr ša I-din-ni.*

[25] Ebeling's dating of this document in the reign of Adad-nirâri I on the basis of the *lîmu*, Aššur-ériš, (*Urkunden*, page 75) is, of course, impossible The name of *Iddin-Kubi mâr Rîš-Nabû* is clearly to be read in line 4 (thus, also, Ebeling, *Eigennamen*, page 44) Unless the business career of Iddin-Kubi extended over more than seventy years, therefore, this Aššur-ériš cannot be the *lîmu* of, e g , *KAV* 96, which belongs to the reign of Adad-nirâri I On the dates of Iddin-Kubi, see below, pages 221 f

[26] Probably, therefore, this document and *KAJ* 163 may be dated more exactly than is attempted by Ebeling (*Urkunden*, pp 79 f)

[27] On the other hand, *KAJ* 263, 10 is not to be restored to
ša ^{âl} *[I]-din-[ni]*

C. Additional documents, based on parallels with *KAJ* 99.

28. *KAJ* 24. Cf. the debtor, *Adad-pılaḫ mâr Mâr-Idıgla mâr Rîš-Nabû* (line 5) and the witness of *KAJ* 99, 23.

29. *KAJ* 163; 65; 28.

a) In *KAJ* 163, also, *Adad-pılaḫ mâr Mâr-Idıgla* appears as witness (line 32).[28]

b) All three documents have the same *lîmu*, given as follows:

KAJ 163, 37: *^{md}A-šur-mu-ta-kıl mâr ^{d}A-šur-[daįįân]*
KAJ 65, 29 f.: *^{md}A-šur-mu-ta-kıl mâr ^{md}A-šur-daįįân*
KAJ 28, 29: *[A-š]ur-mu-ta-kıl.*

That the same *lîmu* is intended by *KAJ* 28 is shown by the parallels between *KAJ* 28 and *KAJ* 151, since *Kînıįa mâr Nûr-Kubı* is the creditor of *KAJ* 28 (line 5), and the recipient of forfeited land in *KAJ* 151 (line 11).

30. *KAJ* 58. In this tablet, also, *Kînıįa mâr Nûr-Kubı* (lines 4 f.) is the creditor.

Since the tablet belongs in this period, lınes 33 f. are doubtless to be restored:

[lı-mu ^{m}Adad-]mu-še-zı-[ıb] (line 34) *[mâr Šu]-zu-ub-^{d}[Marduk].*

Adad-mušêzib is known to have served as *lîmu* during this reign (see above, p. 199, s. v. *KAJ* 13; 161).[29]

31. *KAJ* 23. The appearance of *Iqîšeįa mâr Šıme-nada* (rev. 3) as witness and of *Ṣıllı-Kubı mâr Iqîšeįa* as credıtor (lıne 4) shows this tablet to be a contemporary of *KAJ* 163, where Iqîšeįa is the debtor (line 3) and Ṣilli-Kubi is a former creditor (line 16).

on the basıs of these tablets, as ıs tentatively suggested by Ebelıng (*Eıgennamen*, page 44) *KAJ* 263 wıll be shown to have orıgınated ın the reıgn of Tukultı-Nınurta, and the supposed parallel wıth these tablets ıs therefore impossıble (see the succeeding chapter for the precıse details)

[28] Cf note 26, above.

[29] Thus Ebelıng, *Eıgennamen, s v* Šuzub-Marduk (2), page 89, but contrast *ıbıd* , page 9, *s v* Adad-mušêzıb (1)

D. Additional documents dated by parallelism with *KAJ* 36.

32. *KAJ* 154. This tablet reveals parallels both to *KAJ* 36, a document of the reign of Aššur-uballiṭ, and to *KAJ* 1, a document which probably comes from the reign of Erîba-Adad. All three documents mention a certain *Anniịa* (*Annuịa*) *mâr Šamaš-âmeri*. In *KAJ* 1 (line 2), he gives up his son for adoption. In *KAJ* 36 (line 13), he appears as witness. In *KAJ* 154 (line 5), his field is mentioned to define a tract of land dealt with in the contract

That the same person is intended in all three documents is reasonably certain. The name appears in the following forms:

KAJ 1, 2: *^{m}A-ni-ịa mâr ^{d}Šamaš-a-me-ri*
KAJ 36, 13 [*^{m}A-n*] *i-ịa mâr ^{d}Šamaš-a*!*-me-ri*
KAJ 154, 5 f. . . *^{m}An-nu-ịa* (line 6) *mâr ^{d}Šamaš-a-me-ri.*

The only doubtful identification would be the last; but since there are other parallels between *KAJ* 154 and documents of this period, the element of doubt cannot be very serious. However, on the basis of one additional parallel, it is preferable to date *KAJ* 154 in the reign of Aššur-uballiṭ rather than in the reign of Erîba-Adad:

Nîr-Tašmetum mâr Aḫu-illika, a witness to this document (line 22) is the debtor of *KAJ* 58 (lines 6 f. Cf. also *KAJ* 150, 21). Moreover, Abi-ilu, the father of Šamaš-šêzib, the seller of the land involved in this transaction, is, most likely, the same Abi-ilu, who witnesses *KAJ* 36 (line rev. 1), the father of both men being named Bêlšunu. It is unlikely, though not impossible, that the activity of the son should take place much before that of his father.[30]

33. *KAJ* 41. This document is an approximate contemporary of *KAJ* 154, since both documents mention, as a witness, a certain *Šumu-libši mâr Urad-Tešup*.

[30] Ebeling uses the parallel with *KAJ* 58 to date the document in the reign of Aššur-uballit (*Urkunden*, page 57), without mentioning the possibility of dating the tablet on the basis of the parallel with *KAJ* 1 and *KAJ* 36 In spite of this, he does not identify the Abi-ilu of *KAJ* 153, 155, etc , with the father of Šamaš-šêzib in this tablet (*Eigennamen*, page 5).

In *KAJ* 154, his name is written· (line 23) *Šumu-lıb-ši mâr Urad-Te!-šup* [31]
In *KAJ* 41, we are to read·[32] (line 18) *Šumu-lıb-ši mâr Ar-dı-Te!-šup!*

34. *KAJ* 135. Both *KAJ* 135 (line 3) and *KAJ* 154 (line 4) define land on the basis of the *âlı ša* ᵐ*Lıtılu*. *KAJ* 135 thus belongs, very roughly, in this period.

35. *KAJ* 70.[33] *Abı-ılu mâr Bêlšunu*, who witnesses this document (line 20) is witness, also, to the transaction of *KAJ* 36 (cf. line 13)
Cf., also, *KAJ* 152, 23; 153, 23; 155, 23 [34]

---

[31] This reading was suggested by J Lewy Ebeling has copied the text and transliterated to read
ERUM-(d)še-ru (*Eıgennamen*, page 19)

[32] Again on the suggestion of Lewy We are not convinced of Ebeling's reading of Aššur-muštêpiš as the *lîmu* of *KAJ* 69, whereby he makes this tablet, also, a contemporary of *KAJ* 41 (*Eıgennamen*, page 26) The traces seem to accord better with Ebeling's alternate suggestion of Aššur-pûtı (*ıbıd*, page 27)

[33] We cannot find ın *KAJ* 70, 21 the traces of the name *Šamaš-dayyân mâr Iqîš-Marduk*, whom Ebeling identifies with the witness of *KAJ* 95, 18 f (*Eıgennamen*, page 82) In the first place, the spelling *da-an* would be unusual, if possible, for *dayyân* The prevailing spelling in these texts is *DI KUD* It is true that the spelling ᵐᵈ*A-šur-da-a-an* occurs ın *KA V* 168, 24, and Ebeling conjectures the reading
ᵐ*Şıllı-*ᵈ*Marduk mâr Da(?)-ıa(?)-nı*
for *KAJ* 96, 3 However, it is not certain that the names formed with *dân* are contractions of names ın *dayyân* We have no basis, for example, for the identification of
ᵐᵈ*Šam-šı-lu-da-a*[*n*] (*KAJ* 250, 2)
and
ᵐᵈ*Šamaš-lu-da*[*yyân*] (written *DI* [*TAR*], *KAJ* 310, 36)
Even assuming the possibility of this spelling, however, the sign between *UD* and *DINGIR* ın *KAJ* 70, 21 does not look like the remnant of a *"da"* Nor can the traces of the father's name be ın any way construed as the remnants of any spelling of [*ıqî*]*š-(d*?)*marduk* It is significant that Ebeling, although venturing this guess under the heading "Šamaš-daıân" (*Eıgennamen*, page 82), does not repeat the possibility under the heading Iqîš-Marduk (*ıbıd*, page 49)
Thus we shall not venture to date *KAJ* 95 on the basis of this alleged parallel with *KAJ* 70

[34] Perhaps, also, we should read the name of the first witness of *KAJ* 21

E. An additional document dated on the basis of a parallel with *KAV* 212 and *KAJ* 6.

36. *KAJ* 143 (?). Aššur-kîna-idi, the *lîmu* of *KAV* 212 and *KAJ* 6, may be mentioned in *KAJ* 143, 12 (*a-na bît ᵈA-šur-ki-na-i-di*).

III. The following documents may be dated either in the reign of Erîba-Adad or in the reign of Aššur-uballiṭ. The evidence does not permit us to make a more precise estimate of their date.

1. *KAJ* 35. N. B. lines 30 f., to be read either:
li-mu [E-ri-ba -ᵈ]Adad uklim^{lim}; or:
li-mu [. . . . mâr E-ri-ba -ᵈ]Adad uklim^{lim}.

In the latter case, the tablet might belong to the reign of Aššur-uballiṭ.[35]

2. *KAJ* 146. Ebeling tentatively suggests the reign of Erîba-Adad as the time of origin of this document by identifying one of the witnesses as a witness to *KAJ* 35 (*Urkunden*, p. 59).

Thus, we read with Ebeling in *KAJ* 35, 26. [*Urad-K*] *u-be mâr Nûr-Ku-be* (cf. the name of the seal-owner in line 23), who is to be identified with the witness in *KAJ* 146, 20.

As a matter of fact, the documents are much more closely related than Ebeling indicates.

a) Both documents involve an area of 30 *ikû* of land situated in the same district — in *KAJ* 35, *ugâr* [*Pu-ra-*]*dá-ti* (line 11), and in *KAJ* 146, *ugâr Pu-ra-da-ti*.

b) Innasḫira, the debtor of *KAJ* 35, is merely a variant form of Ili-nasḫira, the debtor of *KAJ* 146. The remaining parallels will make this identification certain. Although

as *A-bi-ilu mâr* [*B*]*êl*-[*šu-nu*] (thus Ebeling, *Eigennamen*, page 5) *KAJ* 21 is not dateable on the basis of any other of the proper names mentioned It is only by guesswork, therefore, that we may identify this witness with the *Abi-ilu mâr Bêl-šunu* of *KAJ* 36, etc (For a full discussion of the role of Abi-ilu, and the reading in *KAJ* 21, see below, page 217)

[35] Contrast Koschaker, *op cit*, page 7, where only the former possibility is considered

Ebeling suggested *Il-nasḫira* as the etymology of *Innasḫira* (*Eigennamen*, p. 48), he does not identify the persons so named in *KAJ* 35 and *KAJ* 146 respectively.

c) The scribe of both tablets is the same. *KAJ* 35, 27 f. seems to read:
[. . . .]-*a-tu-qa tupšarr*[*um mâr E-ri-i*]*b*-^{d}*Sîn-na.*

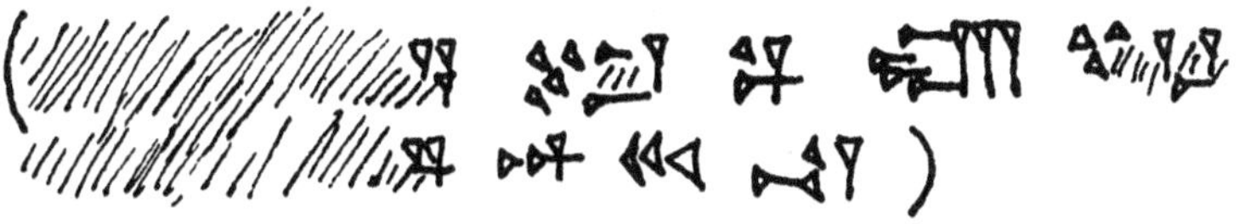

KAJ 146, 22 f., reads:

mâr E-rib-Sîn-na.

It is likely, however, that the first sign preserved in *KAJ* 35, 27 is the latter part of the  sign, and that the sign copied by Ebeling as a somewhat scatched "*tu*" is, in actuality, a partially erased "*dam.*"

Thus, we are inclined to read *KAJ* 35, 27 f. in the same way as *KAJ* 146, 22 f.: [*maḫar Ša*-^{d}*A-šu*]*r-dam*!-*qa tupsarrum* [*mâr Erib*]-^{d}*Sîn-na.*

d) We should also read in *KAJ* 35, 24: [*maḫar In-na-me-ir*] *mâr Šu-ru-ri-a* (cf. *KAJ* 146, 21).

To be sure, the trace remaining there in the left-hand-side margin is troublesome. The name mentioned here apparently begins with a *Ia*, and we should expect, according to our present reconstruction, a reference either to Innamir or else to the scribe. Since, however, the text is so poorly preserved, this one sign cannot be considered a serious obstacle to the suggested reconstruction.

Assuming that these identifications are correct, then the participants in *KAJ* 35 and 146 are identical in the following respects the mortgagor is the same, the scribe is the same; and the witnesses are the same, except that *KAJ* 35 has one additional witness (line 25). It seems clear, therefore, that the documents deal with the same transaction, and that the name of *Iddin-Kubi mâr Rîš-Nabû* must be supplied in *KAJ* 146, line 10. *KAJ* 35 acknowledges a loan made by Innasḫira from Iddin-Kubi, the security for which consists of 30 *ikû* of his land. *KAJ* 146 acknowledges the transfer of this land to Rîš-Nabû mâr ili-nasḫira.[36]

3. *KAJ* 38. The witness of lines 21 f., *Urad-Tašmetum mâr Mâr-Šerua*, is probably intended in *KAJ* 35, 25, which is then to be read. [*maḫar Urad*]-*ᵈTaš-me-tum mâr Mâr-ᵈ*[*Še-ru-a*]. If this is so, *KAJ* 38 and 35 are approximate contemporaries. Undoubtedly, also, *KAJ* 35, 23 and *KAJ* 35, 25 both refer to the same Urad-Tašmetum (cf. Ebeling, *Eigennamen*, pp. 19 f.).

IV. The following document is to be assigned to the reign of Enlil-nirâri:

KAJ 156 (N. B line 36; cf. Koschaker, *op. cit.*, page 7) [37]

Part 2 — The Career of Bêl-qarrâd

The transactions of *Bêl-qarrâd mâr Urad-Kubi* are preserved in five tablets (*KAJ* 33; 34; 41; 43; *KAV* 209), which may be dated in the reign of Erîba-Adad and in the early years of his successor, Aššur-uballit The documents record the obligation of various debtors to repay specific quantities of lead to Bêl-qarrâd.

[36] If the same Innasḫira is the father of Šamaš-šar, a witness to the transaction in *KAJ* 66 (line 36), then Piqabaiašea, the debtor in *KAJ* 66 may well be the brother of Innasḫira (the debtor in *KAJ* 35 and 146) The father of both men is named Apapa (*KAJ* 66, 4 f , 146, 9) It seems not unlikely that a nephew of the debtor should witness a transaction for the creditor, and it is therefore to be assumed that the Iddin-Kubi mentioned as creditor in *KAJ* 66, 10, 22, is the same *Iddin-Kubi mâr Rîš-Nabû* whom we meet in many contemporary documents It is surprising that Ebeling does not suggest the possibility of this identification (*Eigennamen*, page 44)

[37] For chronological reasons, Ber-ili, the father or grandfather of the debtor of this tablet, cannot be the dignitary mentioned in *VAT* 16380, line 10, etc Contrast Weidner, *AfO*, XIII, page 116

1. The following document in which Bêl-qarrâd is the creditor may be dated in the reign of Erîba-Adad:

   KAV 209 (see above, p. 195).

2. The following document in which Bêl-qarrâd is the creditor comes from the beginning of the reign of Aššur-uballiṭ:

   KAJ 41 (see above, pp 210 f).

3. The following consideration corroborates this dating of the Bêl-qarrâd tablets. *KAJ* 17, a document of *Kıdın-Adad mâr Iddın-Kubı*, mentions the son of Bêl-qarrâd (*Bêl-nâdın-aḫḫê mâr Bêl-qarrâd mâr Urad-Kubı*) as the debtor. Since *KAJ* 17 belongs to the reign of Aššur-uballiṭ, this would confirm the indication that the reigns of Erîba-Adad and Aššur-uballiṭ were the period of activity of Bêl-qarrâd.

The following additional documents of Bêl-qarrâd may therefore be set in the years of Erîba-Adad and Aššur-uballıṭ.

1. *KAJ* 33
2. *KAJ* 34
3. *KAJ* 43.

The following additional documents have the same *lîmu* as *KAJ* 43, and are therefore contemporary:

4. *KAJ* 16 [38]
5. *KAJ* 134 [39]
6. *KAJ* 294.

---

[38] *KAJ* 314 is not to be dated on the basis of *KAJ* 16 There is no reason to suppose that *Ilı-ıqîša mâr Enlılıa*, a witness to the transaction of *KAJ* 16 (line 19), is the same man as is mentioned without patronymic in *KAJ* 314, 2 (Cf Ebeling, *Eigennamen*, page 46) On the dating of *KAJ* 314, see the following chapter

[39] Ebeling reads the *lîmu* of this tablet·

Adad- ³ ⁴ *mâr Bêl-naṣır* (*Eigennamen*, page 32, s v Bêl-naṣır) A comparison with the other tablets, however, reveals that the *lîmu* is to be read Ilu-erıš Compare

KAJ 16, 25 . . .

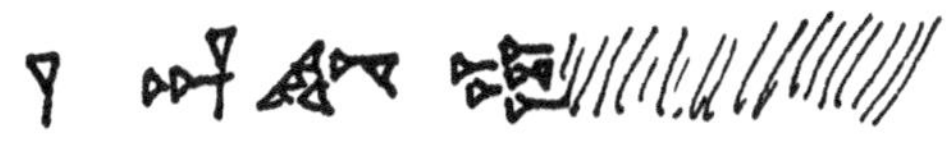

KAJ 43, 21 . . .

In addition to the above, the following tablet, which mentions a participant of two of the Bêl-qarrâd documents, is also of the same general period of origin:

7. *KAJ* 45.

Since, however, *Aḫu-illika mâr Kišati* is mentioned in *KAJ* 34 as the debtor (line 5), in *KAJ* 41 as a witness (lines 16 f.), and in *KAJ* 45 as the creditor (line 4), the last mentioned document may be considerably older or considerably younger than the two Bêl-qarrâd tablets.

Part 3 — The Family of Nûr-Kubi

Nûr-Kubi mâr Bêlšunu, together with several of his sons, was likewise an important figure in the commerce of this period. The transactions of his family are of a more varied type They include not only the loan of lead (*KAJ* 28) and grain (*KAJ* 58, 70), but also the purchase of land (*KAJ* 152; 153; 154; 155). On at least two occasions, a certain Šamaš-tukulti sold areas of his property to the family, once to Nûr-Kubi himself (*KAJ* 153) and once to Eriš-ili and his brothers, the sons of Nûr-Kubi (*KAJ* 155). It seems clear that Šamaš-tukulti had become indebted to Nûr-Kubi, and that his land had been the security. When he was unable to meet his obligation, the land was transferred, in one case to Nûr-Kubi, and in another case to his heirs (see above, pp. 212 ff., for a similar instance of default).

It is not difficult to show that all of these tablets deal with transactions of the same family The sons of Nûr-Kubi mentioned

---

KAJ 134, 20 f . . . . 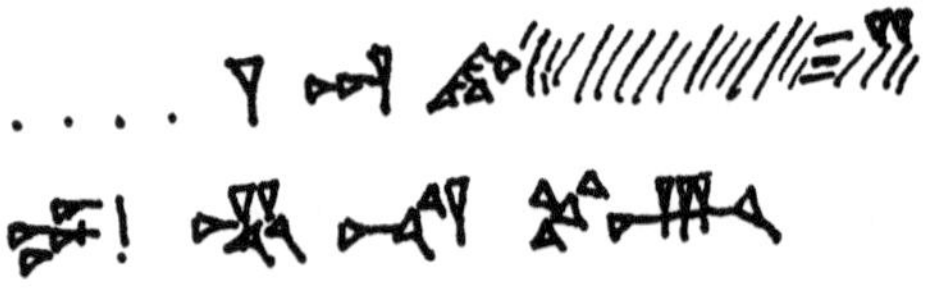 (l 21)

KAJ 294, rev 8 f. . . . .  (l rev 9)

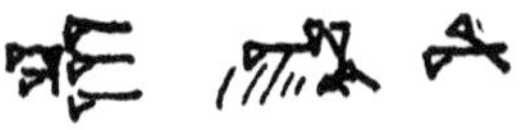 Cf Weidner, *AfO*, XIII, page 315

in *KAJ* 155, who receive land from a debtor of *Nûr-Kubı mâr Bêlšunu* himself, are clearly the heırs of his family. A different son is attested in *KAJ* 70 and 154. That *KAJ* 70, lines 4 and 15 are to be reconstructed on the basis of *KAJ* 154, 11 seems reasonably clear. Thus we read:

(line 4) *ša* [*I-ia-e mâr Nûr-Ku-be*] (note the traces of the first name),

and

(line 15) *i-na bît* ^{m}*I-ia-e*![40]

Thıs reconstruction is made probable by the following facts:

1. Both *KAJ* 70 and 154 can be related to the Nûr-Kubi tablets through the personality of *Abı-ilu mâr Bêlšunu.* Presumably the brother of Nûr-Kubi, Abi-ilu, acts as witness for many of these documents, his name invariably standing first among the witnesses (*KAJ* 152, 23; 153, 22 f ; 155, 23 f) The name of Abı-ilu appears in the same position in *KAJ* 70 (lines 19 f); whereas his son, Šamaš-šêzib (line 9), is the seller of land ın *KAJ* 154.[41]

2. *Nîr-Tašmetum* (*mâr Aḫu-ıllıka*) appears as wıtness both to *KAJ* 70 (line 22) and to *KAJ* 154 (line 22). Thus it is not improbable that the tablets are related Moreover, Nîr-Tašmetum is known to have borrowed grain from Kinniia, another son of the same Nûr-Kubi, as is shown below (*KAJ* 58, 1, 8). Thus, the tablets are once again connected with the family of *Nûr-Kubı mâr Bêlšunu.*

3. The debtor of *KAJ* 70 is most probably the same Šamaš-tukulti, who was ınvolved ın transactions with Nûr-Kubi and

[40] Contrast Ebelıng, *Eıgennamen, s. v Iası*, page 43

[41] *Abı-ılu mâr Bêlšunu* ıs chosen as wıtness to *KAJ* 36 (lıne rev. 1) for an apparently dıfferent reason In thıs tablet, the famıly of Nûr-Kubı does not seem to be ınvolved But Abı-ılu was probably a neıghbor of the borrower of lead, *Šamaš-âmerı mâr* [ ]-*Adad*, and he may have been avaılable for thıs reason (See *KAJ* 154, where the land sold by hıs son ıs defined ın lınes 5 f as beıng ın the vıcınıty of the land of *An-nu-ia mâr* ^{d}*Šamaš-a-me-rı*. That the same *Šamaš-âmerı* ıs ıntended follows from the sıgnature ın *KAJ* 36, rev 2, where the wıtness, presumably the son of the debtor, appears as [*An-n*] *i-ia mâr Šamaš-âmerı*)

another of his sons, Eriš-ilu (*KAJ* 153, 15; 155, 7). Once again, the text of *KAJ* 70 is not well preserved, but the following comparison should be made:

KAJ 70, 5. *ı-[na] mu-[ḫı ᵐ]ᵈ*

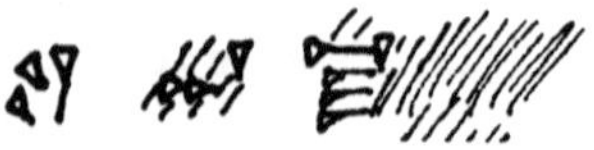

(line 6) [*mâr*]

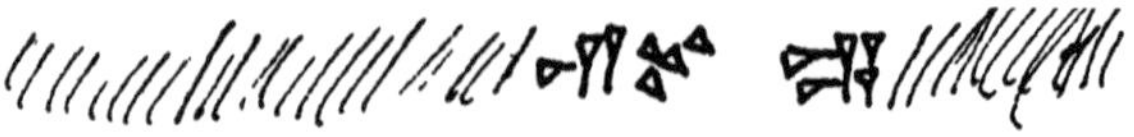

(line 14) *aššat-su ša*

Evidently, the sign following "šamaš" in both versions of the name was read differently by Ebeling, and it may be presumed that neither was distinctly preserved in the original. The reconstruction

(line 5) *ı-[na] mu-[ḫı ᵐ]ᵈŠamaš-[tukultı!]* (line 6) [*mâr Uz-] zı-e* fits well with the remaining traces, and can be regarded as fairly certain.

4. A further son of Nûr-Kubi, Šamaš-bêl-ilâni, may have been a witness to *KAJ* 70. Once again, as a result of the poor state of the text, a conjecture must be resorted to; and the result, in this case, can be considered no more than a possibility.

It is suggested that line 21 of the text be read as Šamaš-bêl-ilâni mâr Nûr-Kubı. The following is the text given by Ebeling

(line 21)

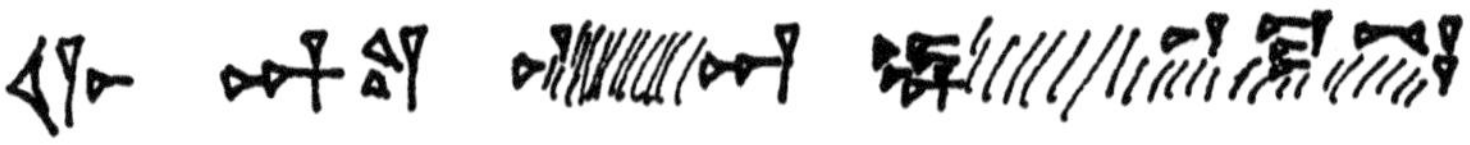

(L. H. M.) [42]

That Šamaš-bêl-ilâni is the son of the same Nûr-Kubi follows from a comparison of *KAJ* 25 and the tablets already mentioned. *KAJ* 25 is the receipt given to *Šamaš-bêl-ilâni mâr*

---

[42] The sign "*EN*" after "*Šamaš*" in the left-hand margin makes Ebeling's reading of Šamaš-d[a]-an difficult For a full discussion, see above, note 33

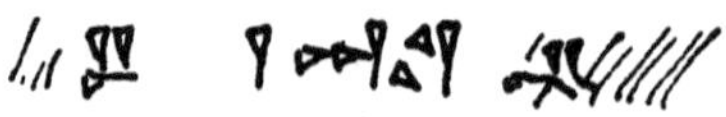

Nûr-Kubi by *Bêl-mušallim mâr Šamaš-uballit* for the loan of a quantity of lead (lines 1–5). The debtor of this tablet appears likewise in *KAJ* 153, 24 and 155, 25, as a witness on behalf of *Nûr-Kubi mâr Bêlšunu* or of his son, *Eriš-ili*. It is natural, therefore, to identify the father of Šamaš-bêl-ilâni with Nûr-Kubi, the son of Bêlšunu.

In addition to these brothers, a further son of Nûr-Kubi appears as a money-lender in our tablets. In *KAJ* 28, 5 and 58, 4 f., *Kinnija mâr Nûr-Kubi* is the lender of quantities of lead and grain; and in *KAJ* 151, 11, as the natural result of such an occupation, he is the purchaser of (forfeited) land. The identification of his father with the Nûr-Kubi with whom we are concerned is made for the following reasons:

1. *Bêl-mušallim mâr Šamaš-uballit*, a witness to *KAJ* 151 (lines 24 f.), and probably father of the witness *Inunu* of *KAJ* 28, 24, is the same man who witnesses *KAJ* 153 and 155.

2. We have pointed out the recurrence of *Nîr-Tašmetum mâr Aḫu-illika* in *KAJ* 58 and 154.

It is clear, therefore, that these four men, all defined in our tablets as sons of a Nûr-Kubi, and all appearing as lenders of lead and grain, are indeed sons of the same man, *Nûr-Kubi mâr Bêlšunu*. In all likelihood, Šamaš-dajjân (*KAJ* 28, 23) is to be added to the group, since, as we have seen, relatives of both creditor and debtor are frequently called upon to act as witnesses. In this case, the creditor is *Kinnija mâr Nûr-Kubi*, while the witness appears as *Šamaš-dajjân mâr Nûr-Kubi*

Two of these brothers, Kinnija and Eriš-ili, strongly remind us of the "adoption papers" preserved in *KAJ* 6, a document in which the son of a certain Eriš-ili is adopted by a certain Kinnija. Although it is not stated that this Kinnija is the uncle of his adopted child, we know of a similar contemporary case (*KAJ* 1), where a child is adopted by his uncle with the permission of the father (lines 1–6). Both Anija, the father of Gimillu, and Azukija, his adopted father, are sons of Šamaš-âmeri.

In confirmation of the fact that we are dealing, in *KAJ* 6, with these same two sons of Nûr-Kubi, it should be noted that two of the witnesses of *KAJ* 6, *Iâkku-limmir mâr Uššur-ana-Marduk* (lines 27 f.) and *Ber-uballiṭ mâr Šamaš-uballiṭ* (lines 30 f.), appear in two documents indirectly related to the transactions of Nûr-Kubi, *KAJ* 36 (line 4) and *KAJ* 150 (line 20), respectively. Laqîpu, who was obliged to sell land in *KAJ* 150 (line 12), likewise sold land to Nûr-Kubi (*KAJ* 152, 7), whereas *KAJ* 36 is distinguished by having as witness *Abi-ilu mâr Bêlšunu*, the brother of Nûr-Kubi

TABLE III

THE GENEALOGY OF NÛR-KUBI

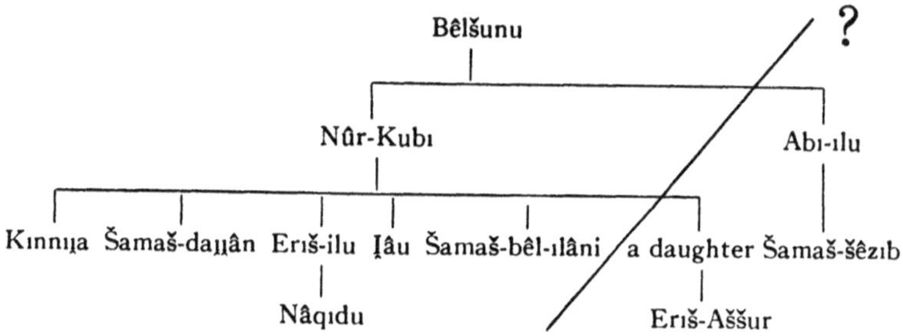

Chronology.

In the previous pages, all of these tablets of Nûr-Kubi and his sons have been dated in the reign of Aššur-uballiṭ.

If Ebeling is correct in reading Abi-ilu mâr Bêlšunu as the first witness of *KAJ* 21 (lines 26 f.), it is conceivable that this tablet, also, represents a transaction of one of the family of Nûr-Kubi (see note 34). In this case, we might restore lines 7 f.:

[*iš-*]*tu Eriš-Aššur* [*mâr* . . .] (line 8) *mârat Nûr-*[*Ku-bi*?].

Such a restoration is questionable, but if it is to be maintained, it would afford us a criterion for dating *KAJ* 21 in the reign of Aššur-uballiṭ.

Part 4 — Iddin-Kubi and his Son

Iddın-Kubı mâr Rîš-Nabû and his son, *Kıdın-Adad*, were active in a variety of business ventures. They lent out grain and lead at interest (*KAJ* 13; 17; 19; 53; 61; 63; 67) They were wealthy enough to lease serfs to farmers at harvest time (*KAJ* 99). They bought out loans which had been made by other creditors (*KAJ* 79; 161, 163), and they acquired land which had been set as the security for unpaid debts (*KAJ* 149). We also have the record of the adoption of a daughter by Kidin-Adad (*KAJ* 2) and of his purchase of a slave (*KAJ* 170; *KAV* 211)

1. The following documents in which Iddin-Kubı participates may be dated in the reign of Erîba-Adad·

   a) *KAJ* 14 (see above, page 194)
   b) *KAJ* 20 (see above, page 194)
   c) *KAJ* 52 (probably; see above, page 197)
   d) *KAJ* 179 (see above, page 198).

2. The following documents of Iddin-Kubi belong to the reign of Aššur-uballit:

   a) *KAJ* 11 (see above, page 204)
   b) *KAJ* 12 (see above, page 207)
   c) *KAJ* 18 (see above, page 199)
   d) *KAJ* 26 (see above, page 207)
   e) *KAJ* 29 (see above, page 205)
   f) *KAJ* 60 (see above, page 199)
   g) *KAJ* 150 (see above, page 206)
   h) *KAJ* 157 (see above, page 208)
   i) *KAJ* 165 (see above, page 206)

3. The following documents of Iddın-Kubi belong to the reign either of Erîba-Adad or of Aššur-uballit

   a) *KAJ* 35 (see above, page 212)[43]
   b) *KAJ* 146 (see above, pages 212 ff).

---

[43] Reading ın line 5·
   ıštu I-dın-[Ku-be mâr Rîš-Nabû].

Our evidence shows, therefore, that Iddin-Kubi flourished in the reigns of Erîba-Adad and Aššur-uballiṭ [44] The following additional documents in which he appears may therefore be dated within these reigns

1. *KAJ* 42
2. *KAJ* 66 (cf note 36, above).

D. The documents of *Kidin-Adad mâr Iddin-Kubi*.

Kidin-Adad is the son of the same Iddin-Kubi whose documents were considered in the paragraphs above (cf. *KAJ* 179, 2 f.) To some extent, his business activity overlapped that of his father. But we may assume that in the earliest of these years he acted as agent for his father. We have only two of his documents which are to be placed in the reign of Erîba-Adad. In the first of these, *KAJ* 179 (see above, p. 198), his father presents him with the title to certain property. In the second, *KAJ* 160 (see above, p 194), he purchases a promissory note from the prince, Aššur-uballiṭ. In none of these does he act in his usual capacity as money lender.

All the remaining dateable documents of Kidin-Adad belong to the reign of Aššur-uballiṭ:

a) *KAJ* 13 (see above, page 199)
b) *KAJ* 17 (see above, pages 200 f.)
c) *KAJ* 19 (see above, pages 200 f.)

[44] Koschaker considers only part of the evidence when he dates the career of Iddin-Kubi entirely in the reign of Erîba-Adad (*NRU*, page 5, note 6) The three tablets which he quotes (*KAJ* 20, 29, 35) might have been written in the reign of Erîba-Adad, although *KAJ* 29 is more probably from the reign of Aššur-uballit (see above, page 205), and *KAJ* 35 might come from either reign (see above, page 212) However, the tablets *KAJ* 18 and 60, written during the eponymy of Enlil-mudammiq, show that the career of Iddin-Kubi extended into the reign of Aššur-uballit Moreover, the occurrence in these tablets of the eponymies both of *Ibašši-ilu mâr Aššur-bêl-apli* (*KAJ* 26) and of *Ibašši-ilu mâr Niru-abi* (*KAJ* 12), at least one of which certainly belongs in the reign of Aššur-uballit, brings the matter beyond all doubt

It should be noted, moreover, that the active careers of father and son overlapped, both being represented in the eponymy of *Ibašši-ilu mâr Aššur-bêl-apli* (*KAJ* 26 and 149, respectively) and in that of his namesake, *Ibašši-ilu mâr Niruabi* (*KAJ* 12 and 63, respectively).

d) *KAJ* 53 (probably; see above, pages 205 f)
e) *KAJ* 61 (see above, page 208)
f) *KAJ* 63 (see above, page 207)
g) *KAJ* 67 (see above, page 205)
h) *KAJ* 79 (= *KAJ* 166; page 208)
i) *KAJ* 99 (see above, page 199)
j) *KAJ* 149 (see above, page 207)
k) *KAJ* 161 (see above, page 199)
l) *KAJ* 163 (see above, page 209)
m) *KAJ* 170 (see above, page 199)
n) *KAJ* 229 (see above, pages 206 f)
o) *KAV* 211 (see above, page 199)

The following is the only additional document of Kidin-Adad,[45] and is therefore most likely to be assigned to the reign of Aššur-uballiṭ:

KAJ 2.

As far as may be determined, these tablets constitute the entire representation, within our sources, of the reigns of Erîba-Adad, Aššur-uballit, and Enlil-nırâri.

---

[45] It is difficult to see on what basis Ebeling suggests the reading of Kıdın-Adad as the *līmu* of *KAJ* 269 (*Eigennamen*, page 52) The name of Kıdın-Adad is not attested as a *līmu* in these documents, and the traces in Ebeling's reproduction of the tablet would permit the reading of Kıdın-ılâni (cf *KAJ* 253, etc) or Kıdın-Kubı (cf *KAJ* 29)

TABLE IV

DOCUMENTS AND EPONYMIES OF THE
FOURTEENTH CENTURY

1. The Reign of Erîba-Adad

Tablet No.	Lîmu
KAJ 1	Aššur-[...]
KAJ 14 KAJ 148	Aššur-mušêzib mâr Kidın-Enlıl
KAJ 20 KAJ 183 KAV 93	Aššur-lî mâr Ibašši-ılu mâr Šuzub-ıli
KAJ 25 KAJ 52	Iâkku-limmir[46]
KAJ 176	Aššur-[....] mâr Aššur-rîmanni[46]
KAJ 179	Erıb-Aššur
KAV 209 KAJ 64 (=68)	Aššur-bêl-kala
KAJ 147 KAJ 160	Unstated

[46] Or, conceivably, to be set in the reign of Aššur-uballıt

2. Either Erîba-Adad or Aššur-uballiṭ

KAJ 16 KAJ 43 KAJ 134 KAJ 294	Ili-eriš mâr Bêl-nâṣir
KAJ 34	Adad-dammıq
KAJ 35	(. mâr?) Erîba-Adad, uklum
KAJ 66	ᵐᵈA?[....] mâr ᵈAdad-[....]
KAJ 146	Aššur-[...]
KAJ 33 KAJ 38 KAJ 42 KAJ 45	Unstated

3. The Reign of Aššur-uballıṭ
   a) The following eponymıes are ın chronological order

KAJ 18 KAJ 27 KAJ 60 KAJ 99	Enlil-mudammıq ↓
(KAJ 170	Perhaps Enlil-mudammıq or Adad-mušêzıb) ↓
KAJ 13 KAJ 58 KAJ 161 KAV 211	Adad-mušêzib ↓
KAJ 17 KAJ 19 KAJ 164	Aššur-šum-uṣur ↓
None	Aššur-nâdın-šumê ↓
Uncertain	Ibašši-ilu

b) The sequence of the following cannot be determined.

KAJ 6 KAV 212	Aššur-kîna-ıdı
KAJ 8	Abu-ṭâb mâr Erîba-Adad uklım mâr Aššur-bêl-nišêšu uklım
KAJ 11	Bêl-qarrâd mâr Erıb-ılı
KAJ 12 KAJ 63	Ibašši-ılu mâr Nıruabı
KAJ 26 KAJ 149 KAJ 152	Ibašši-ılu mâr Aššur-bêl-apli
KAJ 142	Ibašši-ılu (one of the above).
KAJ 23	Gimıllu mâr Ibašši-ılu
KAJ 24	Rîmannı-Marduk mâr Tuttıja
KAJ 28 KAJ 65 KAJ 163	Aššur-mutakkıl mâr Aššur-dajjân
KAJ 29	Kıdı-Kubi mâr Ber-nâdın-aḫḫê
KAJ 36 KAJ 173 KAV 210	Adad-nâṣır
KAJ 41	Aššur-muštêpıš
KAJ 53 KAJ 153 KAJ 155	Išme-Aššur mâr Erıb-Aššur (probably)

KAJ 67 *KAJ* 86	*Ṣınâ mâr Aššur-ıddınna*
KAJ 70	[. . .]*mâr Adad*-[. . . .]
KAJ 79 (=166) *CT* 33, 15b	*Amurru-ma-ılı*
KAJ 96	*Dân-Assur*
KAJ 135	*Aššur*-[. . .] *mâr Enlıl*- [*tak*]-*la*-[*ku*]
KAJ 150 *KAJ* 151 *KAJ* 165 *KAJ* 229	*Aššur-iddın* *Aššur-iddina* *Aššur-iddın tupšarru* *Aššur* (!)-*iddin*
KAJ 154	[. . . .]-*še-rıb*
KAJ 157	*Aššur-erıš*
KAJ 175	*Marduk-nâdın-aḫı*
KAJ 2 *KAJ* 21 (?) *KAJ* 61 *KAJ* 143 (?)	Unstated

4 The Reign of Enlil-nirâri

KAJ 156	*Enlıl-nırârı uklum mâr Erîba-Adad uklım*

CHAPTER III

THE THIRTEENTH CENTURY

Even more fully documented in our sources are the hundred years between the reigns of Adad-nirâri I and Tukulti-Ninurta I. In addition to some private transactions, we are introduced to a considerable amount of official business, negotiated in particular by the family of Aššur-aḫ-iddina, as representatives of the government. Some indication of the scope of this material is given on pages 253 f. below.

PART I — GENERAL CHRONOLOGY

I. The following documents may be directly assigned to the reign of Adad-nirâri I:[1]

1 *KAJ* 307. The *lîmu*, Šulmânu-qarrâd (line 4), belongs to the reign of Adad-nirâri (*AKA*, page 12; cf. *AOB*, page 70).

2. *KAJ* 145. The *lîmu* of this tablet, Ša-Adad-nînu (line 17) is given as a *lîmu* of the reign of Adad-nirâri in *KAH* I, 5, 35; II, 34, margin; cf. *AOB*, pages 92, 94. Cf., also, *Bi* 15, 18, 40, 12 (*Symbolae Koschaker*, page 143).

3. *KAV* 96; 107; 194. The eponymy of Aššur-eriš (*KAV* 96, 19; 107, 24; 194, rev. 14) is likewise to be assigned to this reign (*KAH* II, 33, 36, cf. *AOB*, page 74).[2]

[1] With regard to *KAJ* 233, and its case-tablet, *KAV* 207, a date in the reign of Adad-nirâri I has been suggested, on the assumption that line 8 of both tablets is to be read as the eponymy of an Adad-nirâri However, Weidner insists on the reading Adad-ṣeri, on the basis of the text *dIM-GAB ZAB* rather than *dIM-ZAB GAB* (*AfO*, XIII, page 311) Weidner points also to the absence of the title ***uklu***, although this alone would not be definite proof that the king is not referred to (cf , pages 237 ff. below).

[2] The *lîmu* of the reign of Adad-nirâri is given in *AOB*, page 74, as Aššur-šum-eriš, but it is suggested by Ebeling (*ibid* , page 75, note 10) that the same person is intended as appears in our texts The activity of Bâbu-aḫ-iddina (*KAV* 96, 4, 107, 4, 194, 3) makes this dating at least approximately correct (see below, pages 259 ff)

However, the eponymy of Aššur-eriš mentioned in *KAJ* 157 (line 15) is

II. The following tablets may be assigned to the reign of Shalmaneser I:

1. *KAJ* 75. The *lîmu* of this text is given as ^{md}*Šulmânu-ašarid* (line 24). The title *uklum* is not given after his name, and therefore the tablet may belong some time before his accession to the throne, although his first regnal year is not thereby excluded.[3] As a matter of fact, a *lîmu* ^{md}*Šul-ma-nu-ašarid* is known elsewhere as coming from the reign of Shalmaneser (*AOB*, page 154); and a *lîmu* ^{d}*Šulmânu-ašared šarru* is mentioned in *Bi* 13, 16 (*Symbolae Koschaker, loc. cit.*).

The identification of Šulmânu-ašarid as the king of that name is made possible by the appearance as creditor of *Aššur-aḫ-iddina mâr Adad-šar-ilâni* (lines 4 f), the dating of whose activity is discussed below.[4]

To be sure, the name of the *lîmu* is possibly to be read *Sulmânu-qarrâd*. A man of this name is known as the father of Ištar-eriš, who served as *lîmu* in the reign of either Adad-nirâri or Shalmaneser (see below, page 235); and in *Bi* 31, 21, his name is written ^{d}*DI-ma-SAG*,[5] which is precisely the spelling of the eponymy of this tablet. Such, at any rate, is the suggestion of Speiser (*Symbolae Koschaker, loc. cit.*), which would make a date in the reign of Adad-nirâri more likely for this tablet than a date in the reign of Shalmaneser. But it

to be set in the reign of Aššur-uballiṭ, as has already been shown Whether the Aššur-eriš of *KAJ* 251 (line 12) is to be identified with the *lîmu* of the reign of Aššur-uballiṭ or with that of the reign of Adad-nirâri cannot be determined

3 See below, pp 237 ff. on the eponymy of Tukulti-Ninurta, for a similar instance

4 The reading by Schroeder of ^{d}*Šul-ma!-ašarid* as the father of the *lîmu* in *KAV* 119, 18 (cf Ebeling, *Eigennamen*, page 87) seems unlikely on the basis of *KAJ* 124a In agreement with *KAJ* 124a, rev 9 f , the *lîmu* is to be read as

^{md}*Ištar-eriš mâr* ^{d}*Šul-ma-(nu)!-qarrâd*

The tablet is not to be dated, therefore, on the basis of the dates of Shalmaneser

5 The pronunciation is made clear on the basis of *KAJ* 124a and *KAV* 119, where the name appears, respectively, as ^{d}*DI-ma-nu-UR SAG* and ^{d}*Di-ma-UR SAG*

should be remembered that if "*Šulmânu-qarrâd*" can be written as *ᵈDi-ma-SAG*, then "*Šulmânu-ašarid*" can certainly be written in the same way.

2 The following tablets of the eponymy of *Abi-ilu* (*mâr Aššur-šum-lîšir*):

KAJ 119 (see line 24)
KAJ 242 (see rev., line 6)[6]
KAJ 290 (see line 9).

Proof

a) *KAJ* 113 shows that the following three eponymy years occur in succession:

Abi-ilu (*KAJ* 113, 5)[7]
Aššur-âlik-pâni (line 15)
Mušallim-Aššur (line 38).

The *lîmu*, Mušallim-Aššur, however, is known to belong to the reign of Shalmaneser I (*KAH* I, 13, right margin; *AOB*, pages 126, 158).

b) Additional evidence of the date of *KAJ* 290 is given by the fact that Tukulti-Ninurta is mentioned as the son of the king (lines 4 f.).

3. The following tablets of the eponymy of Aššur-âlik-pâni (see item 2, above).

KAJ 62 (see line 24)
KAJ 114 (see line 29).

4. The following tablets of the eponymy of Mušallim-Aššur[8] (see item 2, above):

[6] On *KAJ* 242, cf the discussion of *Assur* 9819, pages 247 ff, below

[7] On this reading, cf. *Weidner*, *AfO*, XIII, page 311

[8] *KAJ* 110, 30 is not to be read, with Ebeling (*Eigennamen*, page 63), as the eponymy of Mušallim-Aššur, but rather.

li-mu ᵐMu-šal-lim-ᵈA[*dad*]

This reading accords better with the slight trace to be found in Ebeling's reproduction of the text after *DINGIR* It is to be preferred for the following reasons:

Urad-Šerua appears, in the eponymy of Mušallim-Aššur (*KAJ* 109, 15 f, 113, 34 f), as an agent in certain official transactions In *KAJ* 113, he is in charge of the royal grain, collected from the town of Amasaki during the two

KAJ 83 (see line 31)
KAJ 109 (see line 23)[9]
KAJ 113 (see line 38)

5. The following tablets of the eponymy of Aššur-kâšid. This eponymy is known to be from the reign of Shalmaneser on the basis of *KAH* I, 15, 29; cf. *AOB*, page 138; and *Bi* 8, 27 (*Symbolae Koschaker, loc cit.*).

KAJ 51 (see line 23)
KAJ 90 (see line 23).

6. *KAJ* 123; 262.[10] The eponymy of these tablets, that of Aššur-dammiq (*KAJ* 123, 14; 262, 20), belongs likewise to the reign of Shalmaneser (see *AOB*, pages 130, 156).

previous years, and he assigns it for ultimate delivery to Aššur-kitte-idi, governor of Naḫur, to be used for the "uprooted men" (*ṣâbê nasḫûte*) of that city In *KAJ* 109, written two days later, Urad-Šerua (lines 15 f) was once again in charge of the royal grain, this time in Naḫur, and he had transmitted it for ultimate delivery to the city of Šuduḫi, once more for the use of the "uprooted men " In these tablets, Urad-Šerua does not appear as one of the principal royal officials who lends grain and money in his own name

On the other hand, in *KAJ* 110, Urad-Šerua has direct authority over large quantities of grain which is lent in his own name Since, during the years surrounding the eponymy of Mušallim-Aššur, both his grandfather, Aššur-aḫ-iddina (*KAJ* 83, 3 f., 62, 3 f) and his father Melisaḫ (*KAJ* 114, 3 f , 119, 6 f) were active in this way, and since we find no similar activity of Urad-Šerua during the time of activity of either his grandfather or his father (see below, pages 256 ff), it seems most likely that *KAJ* 110 is to be set in the reign of Tukulti-Ninurta, in the eponymy of Mušallim-Adad (cf also note 58, below)

[9] The mention of an Assyrian governor of Šuduḫi, which was conquered by Adad-nirâri I (*KAH* I, 5, 10), corroborates this dating

[10] Ebeling presumably reads in *KAJ* 262, 6

[*ša li-me*] *ᵐKi-din-ilâni*$^{meš\ ni}$

(*Eigennamen*, page 53), in which case the dating of *KAJ* 253 (line 11) and 258 (line 8) might be established as the year preceding *KAJ* 262

To be sure, the text of *KAJ* 262, 6–10 is too fragmentary to be reconstructed It seems clear, however, that despite the difference in spelling, the Kidin-ilâni of line 6 is the owner of the seal identified in line 1, and hence in this contract he is the borrower of grain from Aššur-aḫ-iddina Why Ebeling has identified *KAJ* 262, 6 with *KAJ* 253, 11 and 258, 8, rather than with *KAJ* 262, 1, is not clear While it is possible that the debtor of *KAJ* 262 is to be identified with the *lîmu* of the other tablets, there is no evidence to suggest such identification, and the likelihood is not very considerable

The following additional tablets may be dated on the basis of parallels with tablets mentioned in rubrics 1–6:

7. *KAJ* 80. *Aššur-mušabši mâr Aššur-dugul*, who appears as scribe in two documents known to come from the reign of Shalmaneser I (*KAJ* 119, 20 f ; 83, 28 f.[11]), is also the scribe of *KAJ* 80 (lines 29 ff.).[12]

8 The *lîmu*, Enlil-ašarid, of *KAJ* 80 (lines 4,[13] 34), appears as *lîmu* of the following documents, which are therefore to be set in the reign of the same king·

KAJ 115 (line 23)
KAJ 308 (line 12; cf. Ebeling, *Eigennamen*, page 37)
KAJ 311 (line 18)
KAV 103 (line 32)
KAV 203 (line 37).

9. *KAJ* 159; 267. The *lîmu* of these tablets, Eribtaja'u (*KAJ* 159, 18; 267, 24) appears in *KAJ* 80 as the *lîmu* immediately preceding Enlil-ašarid (*KAJ* 80, 2 by collation of Weidner[14]). The Billa texts quoted by Speiser (see below, pages 233 ff.) confirm the dating given in rubrics 7–9.

10. *KAJ* 158. Like *KAJ* 159, this tablet sets forth the responsibilities of Bâbu-aḫ-iddina (*KAJ* 158, 8 f.; 159, rev. 4) to Kurbani (*KAJ* 158, 3 f.; 159, 6) and Nabû-kitte (*KAJ* 158, 7; 159, 5 f.) With so many parallels, we need not hesitate in regarding the documents as almost contemporary.

11. *KAJ* 225. The following parallels connect *KAJ* 225 and *KAJ* 267:

a) Urad-Papsukkal, *nâqidu* (*KAJ* 225, 6 f.; 267, 6)
b) Uṣur-bêl-šarri, *bêl paḫite* (*KAJ* 225, 15 f.; 267, 6)
c) Bunija (*KAJ* 225, 19; 267, 20).

[11] Reading (line 28) [*maḫar* ^{d}*A-šur*]*-mu-šab-ši tupšarru* (line 29) [*mâr A-šu*]*r-du-gul*! (Ebeling, *Eigennamen*, page 25)

[12] Reading (line 29) *maḫar* ^{d}*A-*[*šu*]*r-mu-šab-ši* (line 30) *tupšarrum* (line 31) *mâr* ^{d}*A-šur-du-gul* (*ibid*)

[13] Reading thus with Weidner in line 4 (*AfO*, XIII, page 315).

[14] *AfO*, XIII, page 118

12. *KAJ* 182, 184 The *lîmu* of these tablets, Aššur-kitti-idi (*KAJ* 182, 3; 184, 3), is likewise *lîmu* of *KAJ* 225 (line 22).

13. *KAJ* 171.[15] This tablet is produced by the same scribe, *Erîba-Adad mâr [Rî]manni-Adad* (lines 33 f.) as *KAJ* 114 (N. B lines 26 f.). In addition, it should be noted that *Mardukiia mâr Lulaiae*, who assumes the obligation of *KAJ* 171 (line 4, etc), is a witness to the transaction of *KAJ* 80 (lines 25 f). Both *KAJ* 80 and 114 belong to the reign of Shalmaneser.

14. Speleers No. 314. By collation, the *lîmu* of this tablet has been shown to be *Ber-šum-lîšir* (see *AfO*, XIII, pp 313 f.). An official of this name is known from *KAJ* 113, 7; and on the basis of this fact, the tablet may be approximately dated

15. *KAJ* 275 (?). Perhaps *mKi-[din-Sîn] mâr dAdad-te-ia* may be identified with the *bêl paḫite* of the city of Šuduḫi (*KAJ* 109, line 18; cf. note 9). If so, we should have an indication that this tablet belongs, very approximately, to the reign of Shalmaneser.

16 *KAJ* 121. This tablet is approximately contemporary with *KAJ* 51. The scribe of *KAJ* 51, *Adadteia mâr Ištar*(?)*-šum-eriš*, seems to be mentioned as an *amêlqîpu* (line 13) in *KAJ* 121 (lines 9 f.) The fact that *Melisaḫ mâr Aššur-aḫ-iddina* takes part in both tablets, and that the tablet is still dealing with the "*ṣabê nasḫûte ša alNaḫur*" lends weight to the identification.

III. Still further tablets may be dated in the reigns of Adad-nirâri I and Shalmaneser I on the basis of the excavations of

[15] Schroeder (*MAOG*, IV, pp 201 f) dates this tablet in the reign of Tukulti-Ninurta, on the assumption that Aššur-bêl-ilâni was appointed *lîmu*-officer as a result of his activity (described in *KAJ* 103, 106, and 133) as *bêl paḫite* of Aššur However, although we have no reason to doubt Schroeder's dating of *KAJ* 103, etc (see below, page 241), it remains possible that an official as exalted as the *bêl paḫite* of Aššur had served as *lîmu*-officer some twenty years earlier

The dating of *KAJ* 171 on the basis of *KAJ* 114 and *KAJ* 80 seems cogent, therefore, and there is no objection to ascribing the tablet to the reign of Shalmaneser

Speiser at Tell Billa. Speiser gives the following list of eponyms which can be recovered from tablets found in Level ii of the excavations (*Symbolae Koschaker*, page 143. Transliteration of Speiser).

dA-šur-kāšidid Bi 8, 27
Y *dA-šur-šadû-ni-še-šu Bi* 38, 14
Y *dIštar*(*U-DAR*)-*êreš Bi* 25, 12; 31, 21 (son of *dDI-ma-SAG*)
Y *E-rib-ta-ya-e* (gen) *Bi* 5, 2
Y *Kidin-dSin mâr Adad-te-ya Bi* 9, 25
Y *Kur-ba-nu Bi* 91
[Y *M*]*u-ši-ib-ši-dVII-ta Bi* 6, 27
Y *Ša-dAdad*(*IM*)-*ni-nu Bi* 15, 18; 40, 12
Y *dŠulmânu-ašarēd šarru* (*DI-ma-nu-SAG lugal*) *Bi* 13, 16.

A. The dating of these tablets:

1. Speiser points out that at least eight of these tablets (*Bi* 6; 8; 13; 15; 25, 31; 40; 48) are contemporary, the principal figure of all of them being a certain Sin-apla-eriš Thus, the following eponymy years belong to the same general period·

Aššur-kâšid
Ištar-eriš
Mušibši-Sibîta
Ša-Adad-nînu.

Of these, the eponymy of Aššur-kâšid is known to belong to the reign of Shalmaneser (see above, page 231), whereas the eponymy of Ša-Adad-nînu dates from the reign of Adad-nirâri. It may therefore be assumed that the remaining two eponymy years belong to one of these reigns (thus Speiser, *loc. cit.*).

No doubt, therefore, Speiser is correct in identifying Mušibši-Sibîta with the *lîmu* Mušabšiu-Sîbi of *KAH* II, 41, 28, whose eponymy likewise comes from the reign of Shalmaneser.

2. It is evident that the last mentioned eponymy, that of *Šalmânu-ašarid šarru*, belongs to the earliest years of Shalmaneser (cf. Speiser, *loc. cit.*).

3. The eponymy of Eribtaịau has also been shown to fall within the reign of Shalmaneser (see above, page 232).

4. *Kidin-Sin mâr Adad-teịa* is without doubt the governor of the city of Šuduhi, mentioned in *KAJ* 109, 18 f. Once again, therefore, the reign of Shalmaneser is indicated as the time of origin for these documents (see above, page 231).

B. Conclusions. It is evident, therefore, that the documents of Level ii of the Billa excavations come from the reigns of Adad-nirâri I and Shalmaneser I. On this basis, the following text is dated in the reign of Adad-nirâri:

KAJ 10. *Kurbânu mâr Riše[ịa] mâr Ibašši-ilu*, the *lîmu* mentioned in this tablet (line 2), is probably to be identified with the lîmu of *Bi* 91. Since the father of the *lîmu* mentioned in *KAJ* 10, 2 *Kurbânu mâr Rišeịa mâr Ibašši-ilu*) is one of the participants of *KAV* 212, it follows that *KAJ* 10 cannot, with any likelihood, be earlier than the reign of Aššur-uballiṭ. The dating in the reign of Adad-nirâri, twenty-two or more years later, is more likely than a date in the reign of Shalmaneser, for which at least fifty-four years, and probably more, would have had to elapse between the writing of *KAV* 212 and that of this tablet.

C. The following tablet is to be dated in the reign of either Adad-nirâri or Shalmaneser:

1. *CT* XXXIII 14b. The *lîmu*-officer of this tablet, Aššur-šadû-nišêšu (line 8) is given as the *lîmu* of *Bi* 38, 14.

D. The following tablets are to be dated in the reign of Shalmaneser (the proof of this more exact dating is given below):

1. *KAJ* 124a (see lines rev. 9 f); *KAV* 119 (see line 18). The *lîmu* of these tablets, *Ištar-eriš mâr Šulmânu-qarrâd*, is to be identified with the *lîmu* of *Bi* 25, 12; etc. (Cf. Weidner, *AfO*, XIII, page 118.)

2. *KAJ* 219 (?) (see line 13). The *lîmu* of this tablet, Ištar-eriš, is quite possibly to be identified with the *lîmu*-officer of the above tablets.

3. Weidner points out on the basis of an unpublished text (*Assur* 14410 p) that the following eponymies occur in this order:

Ištar-eriš
Aššur-da'isunu
Usât-Marduk.

(*AfO*, XIII, page 312, *s v.* Aššur-da'isunu). On this basis, the following tablets are to be dated:

a) Eponymy of Aššur-da'isunu
KAJ 124
KAV 156.

b) Eponymy of Usât-Marduk
KAJ 104
KAJ 125
KAV 98
KAV 104.

Concerning the date of these tablets· Since *Urad-Šerua mâr Melisaḫ* is mentioned in one of these tablets (*KAV* 156; see below, page 256), it follows that a date in the reign of Adad-nirâri is excluded. (On the dates of Urad-Šerua, see below, pages 256 f)

4. *KAJ* 48, 223; 310. *KAJ* 223 is roughly contemporary with *KAJ* 124, mentioning in lines 5 f. the same person, Balṭu-kâšid, *aškapu*, as we meet in *KAJ* 124, 2. *KAJ* 48; 223; and 310 were all written in the eponymy of Lulaįau (*KAJ* 48, 22; 223, 14; 310, 68).

5. *KAJ* 217; 314. Weidner points out, on the basis of an unpublished text, that the *lîmu* of these tablets, *Ber-bêl-litte* (*KAJ* 217, 12; *written Ber-bêl-la-itte*, *KAJ* 314, 11) immediately preceded Lulaįau, the *lîmu* of *KAJ* 48, etc , in the exercise of his eponymy (*AfO*, XIII, page 113).

Weidner suggests that *KAJ* 314 cannot be earlier than the reign of Tukulti-Ninurta (*ibid.*, page 111), since all of the place-names mentioned in the tablet are taken from conquests of that king. Martin points out, however, that an earlier date is not to be excluded.[16] On the basis of Adad-nirâri's conquest of Katmuḫi,[17] and of Shalmaneser's mention of an Assyrian conquest of Arina even before his reign,[18] Martin assumed that the tablet comes most probably from the reign of Adad-nirâri. Since, on the basis of the historical evidence, any dating in this general period cannot be precluded, the above suggestion of a date in the reign of Shalmaneser appears to be acceptable.

6. *KAJ* 49. The scribe of this tablet, *Šamaš-šum-eriš mâr Iqîš-Adad* (lines 22 f.) is identical with the scribe of *KAJ* 48 (lines 19 f.). Moreover, *Aššur-mušabši mâr Aššur-dugul*, who appears as the scribe of three documents in the reign of Shalmaneser I (*KAJ* 80, 29 ff.; 119, 20 f ; 83, 28 f), is a witness to the transaction of *KAJ* 49 (lines 18 f.).

7. *KAJ* 59 (?). If the *lîmu* is to be read
(line 24) [*Šamaš-ki*]-*ti-i-di*,
then the tablet is contemporary with *KAJ* 49 (see lines 26 f.).

IV. The following eponymy years may be assigned to the last regnal year of Shalmaneser I and to the reign of Tukulti-Ninurta. Their order is determined by the chronological sequence of *KAJ* 240.[19]

i) *Upru* (*KAJ* 240, 2)[20]
ii) *Tukulti-Ninurta* (lines 4, 12)
iii) *Qibi-Aššur* (lines 13, 19)
iv) *Mušallim-Adad* (line 26).

A. Concerning the eponymy of Tukulti-Ninurta.
The eponymy of Tukulti-Ninurta appears in two forms·

1. as ^{m}*Tukulti-*^{d}*Ninurta* (*KAJ* 138, 15, 312, 15).

[16] "Der Tribut bei den Assyrern," *Studia Orientalia*, VIII, 1, pp 21 f
[17] *AOB* I, page 62.
[18] *Ibid*, page 114.
[19] Cf. Schroeder, *MAOG*, IV, pages 202 f
[20] Undoubtedly also in *KAJ* 138, a tablet of the eponymy of Tukulti-Ninurta, we should read in lines 2 f :
(line 2) . . *ša li-me* (line 3) [*Up-r*]*i* . . . (but cf. *Eigennamen*, page 92).

2. as *^{m}Tukulti-^{d}Ninurta uklum*(^{lum}) (*KAJ* 144, 21; 238, 11; 272, 8).

3. In *KAJ* 240, 12 and *KAV* 196, 14, it is not certain which of these readings is found.

It might be ventured, on this basis, that two different years are involved; the first during the reign of Shalmaneser,[21] and the second being the first full year of the reign of Tukulti-Ninurta. A comparison of the documents, however, shows that this is not the most likely possibility.

1. Concerning *KAJ* 240

a) The eponymy *^{m}Tukulti-^{d}Nin[urta]*, as it appears in *KAJ* 240, 4, immediately precedes the eponymy of Qibi-Aššur (lines 13, 19)

b) *KAJ* 230, written in the eponymy of this Qibi-Aššur (line 14), is a tablet of *Zêr-iqîša mâr Iâkkiịa* (lines 3 f.), involving, also, a certain *Zika-šarriịa* (line 10). *KAJ* 238, which mentions the same two officials, was written in the eponymy of *Tukulti-Ninurta uklum.*

Thus, *KAJ* 240 cannot be too distant in time of origin from *KAJ* 238, and the eponymy of Tukulti-Ninurta which it mentions is most likely to be the same as that of *KAJ* 238.

2. A further indication of the date of *KAJ* 240 comes from the following considerations Undoubtedly *KAJ* 144 and 244 refer to two quantities of lead which are owed by *Aššur-ma-apla-eriš mâr Nusku-aḫ-iddina mâr Ea-iddina*[22] to (*Adad*)-*Zêr-iqîša mâr Iâkkiịa*. The tablets are therefore fairly close in time of origin. However, the *lîmu* of *KAJ* 240, Mušallim-Adad, is, as will be shown below, identical with the *lîmu* of

[21] For a case where the crown prince does, in fact, serve as *lîmu*-officer, see below, page 241, on *KAJ* 128, *KAV* 169

[22] Ebeling's reading of *Adad-aḫ-iddina* in *KAJ* 244, 6 (*Eigennamen*, page 6), rather than the reading of [*Nusku*!]-*aḫ-iddina*, would be difficult to maintain on the basis of the evident parallel with *KAJ* 144 See below, page 251.

KAJ 244. It is apparent, therefore, that *KAJ* 144 and *KAJ* 240 are contemporary documents. Hence, it is reasonable to suppose that the eponymy of Tukulti-Ninurta given in *KAJ* 240 is the same as that mentioned in *KAJ* 144 as that of *Tukultı-Ninurta uklum*.

3. Concerning *KAJ* 138 and 312.

Since Qibi-Aššur appears in these documents (line 10), it seems that they also are contemporary with *KAJ* 240, and are written in the first regnal year of Tukulti-Nınurta. The two tablets, involving the same transaction, are quite fragmentary, and the precise position which Qibi-Aššur occupies is not clear.

4. Concernıng *KAV* 196. If the eponymy of *KAJ* 138 and 312 is not to be distinguished, by the absence of the term *uklu*, from the eponymies which mention this royal title, it is unlikely that *KAV* 196, whether mentioning the title or not, is to be so distinguished.

B. Concerning the eponymy of Mušallim-Adad. This eponymy also appears in two forms:

1. as $^m Mu$-$šal$-$lım$-$Adad$ (*KAJ* 122, 20, 240, 26)[23]

2. as $^m Mu$-$šal$-$lım$-$Adad$ $mâr$ $^d Šul$-ma-nu-$qarrâd$ (*KAJ* 241, 14 f.) or [$^m M$]u-$šal$-$lım$-$^d A$[dad] (!) $mâr$ $Šul$-ma-nu-$qarrâd$ (*KAJ* 244, 19 f.).

In this case also, however, both forms of writing refer to the same year. *KAJ* 241 and 240 can be shown to be contemporary by the following comparisons:

a) *KAJ* 240 is written in the year succeedıng the writing of *KAJ* 230, since it mentions the eponymy year of the latter (*Qıbı-Aššur*, line 14) in its enumeration of sums of money accumulated in the course of three years (*KAJ* 240, 13, 19).

b) *KAJ* 230 (see line 3), like *KAJ* 241 (see line 3), is a document of Zêr-iqîša, and they are thus approximately contemporary.

---

[23] On *KAJ* 110, see note 8, above

It is reasonable, then, to assume that the eponymy years of *KAJ* 240 and 241, which must be fairly close together, are actually the same.

C. The documents of this period.

1. The eponymy of Upru.[24]
   KAJ 180 (line 40)
   KAV 106 (line 19)
   KAV 200 (margin)

2. The eponymy of Tukulti-Ninurta:
   KAJ 138 (line 15)
   KAJ 144 (line 21)
   KAJ 238 (line 11)
   KAJ 272 (line 8)
   KAJ 312 (line 15)
   KAV 196 (line 14)

3. The eponymy of Qibi-Aššur:
   KAJ 230 (line 14)
   KAJ 289 (line 17)
   KAJ 291 (line 16)

4. The eponymy of Mušallim-Adad:
   KAJ 110 (line 30)[25]
   KAJ 122 (line 20)
   KAJ 240 (line 26)
   KAJ 241 (lines 14 f.)
   KAJ 244 (lines 19 f.).

V. Documents belonging to the later years of Tukulti-Ninurta.

A. The following documents might theoretically be assigned to the reign of either Aššur-nâdin-apli or of his predecessor, Tukulti-Ninurta. Since, however, *KAV* 169 belongs to a collection of

[24] *KAV* 167, 10 is, of course, to be read ^{m}*Up-ru-*[^{d}*A-šur*] (cf *KAV* 160, 11; 135, 5 Contrast Schroeder in his Introduction, *KAV* page XXIV, and Ebeling, *Eigennamen*, page 92). On the attempt by Ebeling to identify the "*Upru*" of this tablet with the *līmu* of our period, compare, also, note 23 to Chapter II

[25] See above, note 8

tablets from the period of Shalmaneser/Tukulti-Ninurta discussed below (pp. 243 ff.), it is apparent that the earlier of the two possibilities is to be preferred.

1. *KAJ* 128. In line 22, the *lîmu* of this tablet is given as Aššur-nâdin-apli, presumably the king of that name.

2. *KAV* 169. The same *lîmu* is given in line 26 of this tablet.

3. *KAJ* 111. *Urṣa! mâr Iqzu*, the scribe of this tablet (lines 17 f.), is likewise the scribe of *KAJ* 128 (lines 19 f.).

4. *KAV* 168. The *lîmu* of this document, *Aššur-dân* (line 24), is likewise *lîmu* of *KAJ* 111 (line 20).

B. Documents dated on the basis of historical allusion:

1. *KAJ* 103; 106. Schroeder has pointed out[26] that the contents of these tablets, coming from the eponymy of Aššur-zêr-iddina (*KAJ* 103, 19; 106, 19), can be best understood if they are assumed to come from the reign of Tukulti-Ninurta. The

ṣâbê^{meš} *Kaš-ši-e ḫu-ub-te ša* ^{mât}*Kar-du-ni-aš*

(*KAJ* 103, 13 ff.; cf. 106, 10 f.) would be the captives of Tukulti-Ninurta's victory over the Kassites when he established his rule at Karduniaš (cf. *KAJ* 103, 15).[27] The "day of the king" (*KAJ* 106, 13) is, according to Schroeder, the day upon which the captured Kassite king was brought by Tukulti-Ninurta to Aššur.

2. *KAJ* 133. In this tablet (lines 5 f.), as in *KAJ* 103, 5 f.; 106, 5 f., Aššur-bêl-ilâni is the *bêl paḫite* of the city of Aššur.

3. *KAJ* 116. Aššur-bêl-ilâni, the ^{amêl}*qîpu* of the king (lines rev. 9 f.) is probably to be identified with the *bêl paḫite* of Aššur. Since, however, Aššur-bêl-ilâni served as *lîmu* some years earlier in the reign of Shalmaneser (see note 15), it is not impossible that our tablet is to be dated in the earlier reign. As will be shown, the presence of *Urad-Šerua mâr*

[26] *MAOG*, IV, pages 200 ff Cf note 15, above With regard to all these tablets, see below on *Assur* 9819, pages 247 ff.

[27] KAH II, 58, 54 ff.; 60, 60 ff , 61, 34 ff

Melisaḫ, likewise as a royal official (line rev 8), makes both of these dates equally likely.

4. *KAJ* 107;[28] 319. The eponymy of these tablets (*KAJ* 107, 17; 319, 15) is the same as that of *KAJ* 133 (line 17). That *KAJ* 319, 15 f. is to be read

li-mu ^{md}*En-lil-nâ*[*din-apli*] (line 16) *mâr Uš*-[. . . .]

and that this *lîmu* is to be identified with that of *KAJ* 107 is shown by the occurrence as creditor in both documents of Erib-Sîn, *rab alâni* (*KAJ* 107, 2; 319, 2) and as debtor in both documents of Amurru-kitti-idi (*KAJ* 107, 5; 319, 5). It is also possible that Erib-Sin, the *rab alâni* mentioned in *KAJ* 107, 2; 319, 2, served as *lîmu* in the time of Aššur-nâdin-apli, and is mentioned in a document published by Weidner ("Eine Bauinschrift des Konigs Assurnadinapli," *AfO*, VI, page 13). However, the Erib-Sîn of *KAJ* 108, 5 comes from a somewhat earlier period, and there is no valid reason for making an identification in this case. On Weidner's conjecture of a possible identification in both cases, see *ibid.*, page 15.

C. Documents dated on the basis of *T* 232.

In his study of the reign of Tukulti-Ninurta,[29] Weidner quotes an unpublished text (*T* 232), which includes the following lines·

(l. rev. 2) ^{arab}*ḫi-bur ûmu VI*^{kan} *li-mu* ^{Id}*Adad-u-ma-*[*i*]
(l. rev. 3) *napḫar 14 ri-ik-sa-nu sa iš-tu li-me* ^{I} . . .
(l. rev. 4) ^{I}*A-bat-te ù li-me* ^{I}*E-til-pi-i-*^{d}*A-š*[*ur*]
(l. rev. 5) *a-na-*^{âl}*Kar-*^{I}*Tukulti*^{ti}*-*^{d}*Nin-urta ra-ak-s*[*u-ni*]
(l. rev. 6) ^{arab}*ḫi-bur ûmu XIX*^{kan} *li-mu* ^{Id}*Be-ir-*[. . . .].

On the basis of this text, the following tablets may be dated·

1. *KAJ* 301. Since the *lîmu*, Etil-pî-Aššur, is mentioned in the same text as Kâr-Tukulti-Ninurta, it follows that *KAJ* 301, written in this eponymy (line 12), cannot be earlier than the reign of Tukulti-Ninurta. Since *KAJ* 301 is among a group of tablets all of which belong in the reign of either

[28] Republished in the same work as No. 117

[29] "Studien zur Zeitgeschichte Tukulti-Ninurtas I," *AfO*, XIII, page 113.

Shalmaneser or Tukulti-Ninurta (see below, pages 243 ff.), a later date is also excluded.

2. *KAJ* 255 Weidner points out[30] that the text *T* 232, quoted above, mentions two further *lîmu*-years, that of *Erîba-*^{d}*Marduk*[31] and that of *Sa-ar-ni-qu*. It follows that the eponymy of Sarniqu, given in the dating of *KAJ* 255 (line 14), belongs in this general period, and not before the founding of Kâr-Tukulti-Ninurta.

3. *KAJ* 30; 316 (?) On the identification of the *lîmu*, Abattu, of *KAJ* 30, and the *lîmu* of the same name in *T* 232, rev 4, see below, pages 245 f. It is not certain whether the Abattu of *KAJ* 316 is the same person, or his uncle, who served as *lîmu*-officer in an earlier reign Note that, on the basis of *T* 232, the eponymy of Etil-pî-Aššur follows the eponymy of Abattu.

VI. Documents belonging to the reigns of Shalmaneser or Tukulti-Ninurta.

A. Documents dated on the basis of excavation records.

Weidner has pointed out,[32] on the basis of photographs of tablets found in a single group during the same excavation, that the following documents are approximately contemporary.[33]

KAJ 15	*KAJ* 293	*KAV* 168
KAJ 93	*KAJ* 301	*KAV* 169
KAJ 228	*KAJ* 313	*KAV* 201.[35]
KAJ 291	*KAJ* 314	
KAJ 292[34]	*KAJ* 316	

30 *Ibid*, page 117

31 Known from the unpublished text, *Assur*-6045f, see Weidner, *loc cit*

32 *AfO*, XIII, pages 109 ff

33 Together with numerous unpublished texts, some information from which is utilized in this chapter.

34 There is no basis for Ebeling's listing of the Aššur-iddin of this tablet (line 17) together with the *lîmu*-officers of the same name (*Eigennamen*, page 23) Chronological considerations exclude any identification of a person involved in this tablet with persons mentioned in such tablets as *KAJ* 150, or 165 On the dating of *KAJ* 150 and 165, see above, page 206 On *KAV* 135, see note 23 to Chapter II.

35 Whether the Aššur-bêl-apli mentioned in this letter can be identified

However, Weidner's conclusions that all of these documents come from the reign of Tukulti-Ninurta are too far reaching. It will be shown that although a great number of the tablets come from this period, others must be dated less precisely than Weidner believes, while still others may be shown to come from the reign of Shalmaneser, the predecessor of Tukulti-Ninurta.

1. The following documents may be assigned to the reign of Tukulti-Ninurta:

a) *KAJ* 291 (see above, page 240)
KAV 168 (see above, page 241)
KAV 169 (see above, page 241).

b) the following unpublished tablets, referred to by Weidner:

i) *Assur* 11018z. The *lîmu* is given as *Tukulti-Ninurta uklum* (Weidner, *AfO*, XIII, page 114, sub 12), and the tablet thus comes, probably, from the king's first regnal year.

ii) *Assur* 11017w. This tablet comes from the reign of Tukulti-Ninurta, and was written in what was probably his third regnal year. On the eponymy of Mušallim-Aššur, given for this tablet by Weidner (*op. cit.*, page 113, sub 10), see above, page 240.

iii) *Assur* 11018m. On the *lîmu* of Aššur-zêr-iddina (Weidner, *loc. cit.* sub 6), see above, page 241.

c) The following tablet cannot be earlier than the reign of Tukulti-Ninurta.

KAJ 301 (see above, page 243).

2. On the other hand, certain of the tablets of this group are more probably to be assigned to the reign of Shalmaneser.

with the *lîmu* of *KAJ* 257 is altogether uncertain, since the date of *KAJ* 257 cannot be determined on the basis of our present knowledge In any event, he is not the father of Ibašši-ilu, *lîmu* of *KAJ* 26, etc., a possibility which is excluded for chronological reasons On the dating of *KAJ* 26, see above, page 207 Contrast Ebeling, *Eigennamen*, page 22

If Weidner's reading of the *lîmu* of this tablet as *A-bat^1-tu-ma* is correct (*AfO*, XIII, page 311), the full force of the enclitic "*–ma*" is hard to explain.

a) *Assur* 11017n, 11018o. The *lîmu* of these documents is given as *Abattu mar Adad-šumu-lîšir* (Weidner, *op. cit.*, page 112, sub 2). This *lîmu* is to be distinguished from the *lîmu* known from other tablets as *Abattu mâr Adad-šamši.*

Ebeling's publication presents three documents from the eponymy of an Abattu; *KAJ* 30; 89; and 316. The *lîmu* of *KAJ* 30 is given as:

(line 27) *ᵐA-bat-tu* (line 28) *mâr Adad-šam-ši*; the *lîmu* of *KAJ* 89 is restored by Weidner[36] to read:

(line 24) [*ᵐA-ba*]*t-tu mâr*! *Adad*-[*šam-ši*];

and the *lîmu* of *KAJ* 316 is given simply as:

(line 21) *ᵐA-bat-tu.*

It will be shown, however, that *KAJ* 89 cannot be later than the reign of Shalmaneser, whereas *KAJ* 30 belongs, in all probability, to the reign of Tukulti-Ninurta, and is certainly later than *KAJ* 89.[37] Since it is known from *T* 232, rev. 4[38] that the eponymy of one Abattu comes from the reign of Tukulti-Ninurta,[39] it is reasonable to assume that this is the eponymy of *Abattu mâr Adad-šamši*, mentioned in *KAJ* 30. On the other hand, since *KAJ* 89 is perhaps a generation earlier, it must have been written in a different eponymy year. Thus, contrary to Weidner, we restore the *lîmu* of *KAJ* 89:

(line 24) [*ᵐA-ba*]*t-tu mâr*! *Adad*-[*šum-lîšir*].

Moreover, such a hypothesis fits well with Weidner's suggestion that the one Abattu is nephew of the other. We learn from *KAJ* 56 of a *lîmu*, *Adad-šamši mâr Adad-šum-lîšir*. Since *KAJ* 56 belongs in the time of Adad-nirâri

[36] *AfO*, XIII, page 112.

[37] *KAJ* 89 is a tablet of Aššur-aḫ-iddina (reigns of Adad-nirâri/Shalmaneser, see below, pages 254 f.) *KAJ* 30 is a tablet of Zêr-iqîša, who flourished in the reign of Tukulti-Ninurta. Even if the activity of Zêr-iqîša extended back into the reign of Shalmaneser, it could not have been earlier than that of Urad-Šerua, the grandson of Aššur-aḫ-iddina (see pages 252 f. and the chronological tables).

[38] Weidner, *loc. cit.*, p. 112.

[39] See above, page 242.

or Shalmaneser (see below, page 255), it is very likely that the following relationship is to be established:

	Adad-šumu-lîšir		
	↓	↓	
KAJ 56 — *lîmu* of the reign of Adad-nirâri or Shalmaneser	Adad-šamši	Abattu	*KAJ* 89 — *lîmu* of the reign of Adad-nirâri or Shalmaneser
	↓		
KAJ 30 — *lîmu* of the reign of Tukulti-Ninurta	Abattu		

Hence, it is most reasonable to place the unpublished tablets coming from the eponymy of *Abattu mâr Adad-šumu-lîšir* in the reign of Shalmaneser.[40] This consideration enables us, likewise, to find a more accurate date for *KAJ* 89, by excluding the possibility of a date in the reign of Adad-nirâri (see below, page 255).

b) *KAJ* 314. See above, page 236.

c) Moreover, since some of the documents of this group are known to come from the first three regnal years of Tukulti-Ninurta, it does not appear unlikely that others should come from an earlier period There is no *a priori* reason to suppose that the tablets were stored according to regnal years.

d) It should also be pointed out that the eponymy of Uṣur-namkur-šarri (*Assur* 11017g) need not come from the reign of Tukulti-Ninurta (contrast Weidner, *loc. cit.*, page 114). The fact that Uṣur-namkur-šarri is mentioned in a tablet of the time of Tukulti-Ninurta (*VAT* 16381, Weidner, *op. cit.*, Plate VI), does not exclude a year in the reign of Shalmaneser as a possibility for his eponymy.

On the basis of this evidence, therefore, these tablets belong either to the reign of Shalmaneser or else to that of Tukulti-

[40] Contrast Weidner, *op cit*, pages 112 ff If Weidner sets *KAJ* 56 in the time of Shalmaneser on the basis of this family relationship, why not *KAJ* 89 for the same reason?

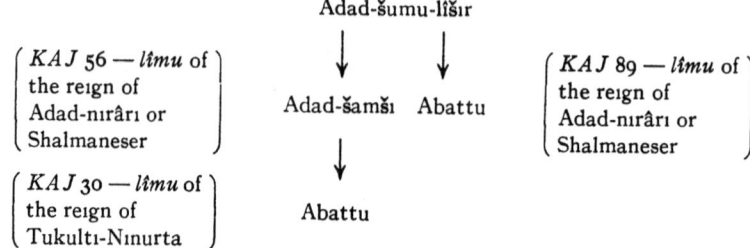

Ninurta. The possibility of a date as late as the reign of Aššur-nâdin-apli is not to be seriously entertained.

The following, then, are the additional tablets dated by this method:

KAJ 15	*KAJ* 293
KAJ 93	*KAJ* 313
KAJ 228	*KAJ* 316
KAJ 292[41]	*KAV* 201

B. Still further documents are to be dated on the basis of a list of royal officials, published by Weidner in the same article on Tukulti-Ninurta (*Assur* 9819 = *VAT* 16380, reproduced as Plate V in the Weidner article). The document itself, as is revealed by the eponymy of Qibi-Aššur (margin), was written during the second year of Tukulti-Ninurta's reign. Once more, therefore, it would be rash to assume that all of the tablets in which one of these dignitaries appears as *lîmu* must belong to the same reign. On the contrary, the possibility of a date in the reign of Shalmaneser, which is not precluded by the dating of *Assur* 9819 itself, is verified by a study of the particular tablets involved. Weidner's dating of all of the tablets in the reign of Tukulti-Ninurta must therefore be regarded only as an approximation.

1. The following documents in which one of these officials participates may be dated, with reasonable certainty, in the reign of Shalmaneser.

   a) *KAJ* 242 (see above, page 230). Compare line rev. 4 with *Assur* 9819, 5 (Nabû-bêl-uṣur).

   b) *KAJ* 171 (see above, page 233). Compare line 36 with *Assur* 9819, 18 (Aššur-bêl-ilâni).

2. The following documents, mentioning officials known from *Assur* 9819, may be dated in the reign of Tukulti-Ninurta·

   a) *KAJ* 111 (see above, page 241). Compare lines 2 f. with *Assur* 9819, rev. 5.

[41] Although the Aššur-iddin mentioned in this tablet may likewise be identified with the official whose name is given in *Assur* 9819, 15, he is certainly

(Ittabši-dên-Aššur, who is mentioned in these places, appears in *KAJ* 111 as the father-in-law of *Urad-Šerua mâr Melimsaḫ*. He is known elsewhere as a *lîmu*-officer; see *KAJ* 279, 12; *KAV* 99, 47; and 205, 39. On this basis alone, however, these three tablets are not to be dated in the reign of Tukulti-Ninurta. It is quite conceivable that here, where Ittabši-dên-Aššur is an active participant, we are dealing with documents somewhat older than *KAJ* 111, which may go back to the time of Shalmaneser. For a fuller discussion of the dating of the eponymy of Ittabši-dên-Aššur, see below, page 263)

Compare, also, *KAJ* 111, 20 and *Assur* 9819, 8 (*Aššur-dân, lîmu*).

b) *KAJ* 107; 319 (see above, page 242). Compare *KAJ* 107, 2; 319, 2 f. (*Erib-Sîn rab alâni*) with *Assur* 9819, rev. 8.

c) *KAJ* 103; 106; 133 (see above, page 241). Compare *KAJ* 103, 6; 106, 5; 133, 5 with *Assur* 9819, 18 (*Aššur-bêl-ilâni*).

3. The following documents, mentioning officials known from *Assur* 9819, may be dated in the general period of Shalmaneser/Tukulti-Ninurta:

a) *KAV* 201 (see above, page 247). Compare the author of this letter, *Gazru* (line 3), with *Assur* 9819, 19.

b) *KAJ* 93 (see above, page 247). Compare line 7 (*Nabû-bêl-uṣur*) with *Assur* 9819, 5.

c) It will be shown below, page 257, that the eponymy of Šunu-qardu (*Assur* 9819, 6) is to be placed in the reign either of Shalmaneser or of Tukulti-Ninurta.

The tablets in which the dignitaries of *Assur* 9819 appear either as *lîmu* or else in some official capacity belong, therefore, within the period of the reigns of Shalmaneser and Tukulti-Ninurta.

not given in this tablet as the *lîmu*-officer Contrast Weidner, *AfO*, XIII, pages 115, 312

4. On the basis of the above reference, the following documents, the *lîmu* of which is Libur-zânin-Aššur (*Assur* 9819, 12) are to be dated in this general period:

KAJ 88 (see line 29)
KAJ 168 (see line 28)
KAJ 218 (see line 11)
KAJ 318 (see line 15)

The dignitary of *Assur* 9819, rather than the *lîmu* Li-bur-[. . . .] of the time of Aššur-uballiṭ,[42] is to be understood. The most compelling indication of this later date comes from a comparison with *KAJ* 116, a tablet which undoubtedly comes from this general period, as is shown by its mention of *Urad-Šerua mâr Melisaḫ* (on his dates, see below). Line rev. 3 of this tablet is to be read:

[Li-bur]-za-nin-ᵈ[A-šur ša] rêš (šarri).[43]

A comparison with *KAJ* 218, 2 f.; 318, 2 f. shows beyond any doubt that the same man is referred to.

On the basis of this suggestion, the following further tablets are to be dated:

5. *KAJ* 263. The parallels between this tablet and *KAJ* 218; 318 are evident. In *KAJ* 263, a load of grain belonging to the palace, under the jurisdiction of *Upru mâr Adad-šum-iddina*, is provided to *Bêl-mušallim mâr Aḫu-ṭâb*, a miller. In *KAJ* 218, grain belonging to *Libur-zânin-Aššur*, the royal representative, once again under the jurisdiction of a man named *Upru*, is given to a different official for the feeding of birds. Finally, in *KAJ* 318, grain of *Libur-zânin-Aššur*, under the jurisdiction of *Upru*, is given to a miller. Without a doubt, the same *Upru* is intended, and hence *KAJ* 263 is to be dated on the basis of these tablets of the eponymy of *Libur-zânin-Aššur*.

On the basis of chronological considerations, it is not unlikely that this Upru is to be identified with the official

[42] Contrast Schroeder, *AK* I, 88 f, and see the discussion of his suggestion, pages 202 f, above

[43] Cf Weidner, *loc cit*, page 115

who served as *lîmu* at the beginning of the reign of Tukulti-Ninurta.

6. *KAJ* 97. Nabû-bêl-uṣur, in *KAJ* 242 (line 8), a tablet of the reign of Shalmaneser, represents the king in the purchase of grain from Bâbu-aḫ-iddina. He appears also in *KAJ* 93, 7, a document of the reign of Tukulti-Ninurta, presumably as an official connected with the *šulmânu* of Šamaš-rîmanni. The same official seems to be the *lîmu* officer of *KAJ* 97 (line 12), although the identification in all three cases is not absolutely certain Thus *KAJ* 97 is possibly to be set, with these tablets, in the reigns of Shalmaneser-Tukulti-Ninurta.

7. Additional Note

Weidner's identification of Aššur-iddin (*Assur* 9819, 15) with the *lîmu* of *KAJ* 150; 165; and 229 (*loc cit.*, page 115) is totally excluded for chronological reasons (see pages 206 f., above, for the dating of these tablets). We have not sufficient evidence to determine whether or not the Aššur-iddin whose name appears on the last line of *KAJ* 292, a document of this general period, is to be identified with the dignitary of *Assur* 9819

Part 2 — Zêr-iqîša mâr Įâkkiįa

Zêr-iqîša appears in these tablets as a man who owns or controls large flocks of sheep Some of his contracts are with shepherds whom he hires to tend the sheep (*KAJ* 127; 230, 238, 271), and other contracts involve loans of lead, grain, or wool, made to various debtors (*KAJ* 30 (?); 59; 144, 241; 244).

A. His Identity.

The name of Zêr-iqîša, as well as his patronymic, appear, in these tablets, in different forms.

1. His name, generally given as Zêr-iqîša, appears in one tablet (*KAJ* 244, 3) as

^{d}Adad-zêr-iqîša (cf. Ebeling, *Eigennamen*, pages 12, 94).

That the same man is intended may be shown by the following considerations:

a) The debtor in two tablets of Zêr-iqîša, including *KAJ* 244, is the same man. Thus, *KAJ* 144, 5 ff. reads

(line 5) ^{md}(*A*!) -*šur*- (*ma*!) -*apla*- *eriš*![44]
(line 6) *mâr* ^{d}*Nusku-aḫ-iddina*^{na}
(line 7) *mâr* ^{d}*E-a-iddina*^{na}

while *KAJ* 244 lines 5 ff. is to be read·

(line 5) [^{md}*A-šur-m*]*a-apla-eriš*[45]
(line 6) [*mâr* ^{d}*Nus*]*ku-aḫ-iddina*^{na}[46]
(line 7) [*mâr* ^{d}*E-a*]-*iddina*.[47]

b) In addition to this parallel, *KAJ* 244 and *KAJ* 241, a further document of Zêr-iqîša, have a common witness,

[44] Cf line 1, for a somewhat more carefully written version of the name

[45] For clear traces of the [. . .-*š*]*ur-ma*, compare line 1 Ebeling's reading of "*Apil-Adad*" in this line (*Eigennamen*, page 17) is without any justification. No such person appears in the tablet; and in this position, we should expect the seal of the man who assumes the obligation. As a matter of fact, the name in line 1 is not difficult to reconcile with the name of the debtor of line 5. The traces of both names are as follows·

(line 1) 

(line 5) 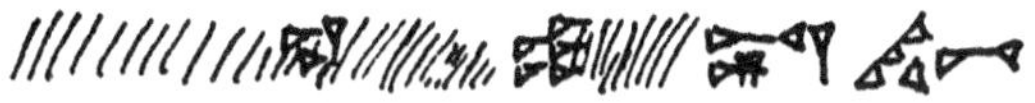

Evidently, the last sign of line 1 is a poorly preserved *KAM*, and in both places the name is to be read

[*A-š*]*ur-ma-apla-eriš*

(Cf , also, a different Ašur-ma-apla-eriš in *KAJ* 241, 5 f)

[46] Ebeling, ignoring the parallel with *KAJ* 144, reads Adad-aḫ-iddina (*Eigennamen*, page 6) The parallel, however, is made even more certain by the designation of the home of the debtor of both tablets as ^{âl}*Lib-bi-âli* (144, 9, 244, 9)

[47] Since Ebeling did not reconstruct *KAJ* 244 on the basis of *KAJ* 144, he did not read the name *Aššur-ma!-apla-eriš* rather than *Aššur-apla-eriš* in *KAJ* 144 The omission of the "–ma" on two occasions in *KAJ* 144, however, need not surprise us (lines 1 and 5) The carelessness of the scribe of this tablet is revealed in other places also In line 5, the "*a*" of *A-šur* is omitted. In line 1, the writing of Aššur (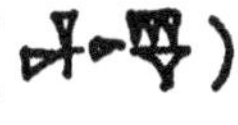) is likewise unusual In the same line, the sign *NITA* is poorly written, and in line 5, the sign *KAM* is completely absent.

namely Šamaš-mudammıq mâr Mušêzıb-Marduk (KAJ 241, 9 f.; 244, 13 f.).

It is clear, therefore, that Adad-zêr-iqîša is the full form of the name of Zêr-iqîša, although the abbreviated form is written in the majority of the tablets.

2. The father of Zêr-iqîša generally appears as Iâkkija. This also, however, may be a hypocoristic form of the full name, Iâkku-limmir, as it appears in KAJ 59, 3 (thus, Ebeling, *Eigennamen*, page 42). Since, however, it is not absolutely certain that the creditor of KAJ 59 is to be identified with the Zêr-iqîša of our remaining tablets, this hypothesis must remain somewhat conjectural.

It is to be noted, however, that such hypocorisma seems characteristic especially of these tablets. For example, an employee of Zêr-iqîša appears in one tablet as

^{m}Zi-qa-šâr-ıli-ı[a] (KAJ 238, 7)

and in another as

^{m}Zi-qa-šâri-ıa (KAJ 230, 10).

We may also conjecture the identification of the scribe in KAJ 30, 24 f. (Šamaš-kimu-abija mâr Mušêzib-Marduk) with the scribe of KAJ 241, 11 (Šamaš-kimuja). Here also, both tablets involve transactions of Zêr-iqîša.

B. The Date of Zêr-iqîša.

1. The following tablet of Zêr-iqîša may possibly be dated, on the basis of the above chronology, in the reign of Shalmaneser I:

KAJ 59 (see lines 2 f.; and cf. page 237, above).

2. The following tablets of Zêr-iqîša can be dated, on the basis of our chronology, in the reign of Tukulti-Ninurta, starting with his first year.

KAJ 30 (see lines 3 f.; page 243, above)
KAJ 144 (see lines 3 f.; page 240, above)
KAJ 230 (see lines 3 f.; page 240, above)
KAJ 238 (see lines 3 f.; page 240, above)
KAJ 241 (see lines 3 f ; page 240, above)
KAJ 244 (see lines 3 f., page 240, above).

The activity of Zêr-iqîša is therefore to be placed perhaps in the last years of Shalmaneser, and chiefly in the reign of Tukulti-Ninurta. On that basis, the following tablets are likewise to be dated in this general period:

1. *KAJ* 127 (see lines 8 f.)[48]
2. *KAJ* 271 (see lines 4 f.).

PART 3 — THE FAMILY OF AŠŠUR-AḪ-IDDINA

The most active participants known to us of the commercial life of Middle-Assyrian Aššur were the three generations of the family of Aššur-aḫ-iddina mâr Adad-šar-ilâni. Koschaker has pointed out[49] that Aššur-aḫ-iddina, his son, and his grandson acted in an official capacity in the economic administration of government. Melisaḫ, the son, is at one time the governor of Naḫur (*KAJ* 109, 10). Among his duties is the provisioning of the "uprooted people" of that town (*KAJ* 121). The grandson, Urad-Šerua, who is known as one of the royal officers (*amlê qi-pu ša šarri*, *KAJ* 116, rev. 10), is given a similar commission for the feeding of the town of *Šu-du-ḫi* (*KAJ* 109; 113).

Some of the private transactions of the family are known to us — the purchase of a house by Aššur-aḫ-iddina (*KAJ* 145), and his order for the building of a chariot (*KAJ* 130). Of a similar nature, perhaps, is the order for bricks given by the wife of Urad-Šerua, which she pays for by means of a letter of credit involving a quantity of wool (*KAJ* 111).

For the most part, however, the transactions are those preserved in the "*šulmânu*-texts," and some related documents. By means of these transactions, lead or gold, grain, livestock, as well as various kinds of slaves were promised as a *šulmânu* to the members of this family. The *šulmânu* is clearly some form

48 It is doubtful whether Bêl-litir, who appears in this tablet (line 12) as a shepherd of Zêr-iqîša (cf *KAJ* 230, line 6), is to be identified with the agent of Bâbu-aḫ-iddina (as is done by Ebeling, *Eigennamen*, page 31) There are no other contacts between the tablets of the two men, and the agent of Bâbu-aḫ-iddina (*KAV* 98, 5, 100, 6) does not appear to be a shepherd The resemblance between the two names is thus coincidental

49 *Op cit*, pp. 138–140.

of official tribute paid to the royal representative. But its precise function is still not clear.[50]

A. The Date of *Aššur-aḫ-iddina mâr Adad-šar-ilâni.*[51]

1. The following tablet of Aššur-aḫ-iddina has been assigned to the reign of Adad-nirâri I:

KAJ 145 (see lines 13 f.; and cf. page 228, above).

2. The following of his tablets belong to the reign of Shalmaneser:

KAJ 62 (see lines 3 f.; page 230, above)
KAJ 83 (see lines 3 f.; page 231, above)
KAJ 262 (see lines 4 f.; page 231, above).

3. The following tablet belongs either in the reign of Adad-nirâri or in that of Shalmaneser:

KAJ 75 (see lines 4 f.; and cf. pages 229 f., above)

The following tablets, then, involving transactions of Aššur-aḫ-iddina, may be assigned to the reigns of Adad-nirâri I and Shalmaneser·

[50] J J Finkelstein (*JAOS*, LXXII, pp 77–80) suggests that the *šulmânu* is a gratuity or bribe, paid in order to secure favorable consideration of a lawsuit

[51] Koschaker's suggestion that the activity of Aššur-aḫ-iddina may belong in the reign of Erîba-Adad (*NRU*, page 8, note 2) is accepted as a possibility by Ebeling (*Urkunden*, page 85). Our chronological conclusions make such a hypothesis untenable Koschaker admits that the *lîmu*, *Aššur-mušêzib mâr Kidin-Enlil* (*KAJ* 14, 27 f , 148, 39 f), need not be the *lîmu* who is given in *KAJ* 98, 28 merely as *Aššur-mušêzib*

Concerning Koschaker's attempt to date *KAJ* 130, on the basis of the eponymy of *KAJ* 123, likewise in the reign of Aššur-uballiṭ, two objections are to be raised:

i) It should not be assumed, without further indication, that the *lîmu* written

^{d}A-šur-da-me-iq (*KAJ* 123, 14)

is to be identified with a *lîmu* written

^{d}A-šur-mu SIG (*KAJ* 130, 21)

ii) *KAJ* 123 is, in any case, to be dated in the reign of Shalmaneser (see above, page 231)

1. *KAJ* 54 (see lines 3 f.)[52]
2 *KAJ* 56 (see lines 3 f.)
3. *KAJ* 76 (see lines 4 f.)
(*KAJ* 81 — see lines 4 f.)[53]
4. *KAJ* 89 (see lines 2 f., to be dated in the reign of Shalmaneser)[54]
5. *KAJ* 98 (see lines 3 ff.)[55]
6. *KAJ* 100 (see lines 16 f.)[56]
7. *KAJ* 130 (see lines 10 ff.)
8. *KAJ* 137 (see lines 5 f.)

B The Date of Melisaḫ, son of Aššur-aḫ-iddina.

All the dateable tablets of Melisaḫ belong to the reign of Shalmaneser, as follows:

KAJ 51 (a transaction of Melisaḫ's wife; see lines 2 ff.; cf. page 231, above)
KAJ 90 (a further transaction of Melisaḫ's wife; see lines 3 f.; cf page 231, above)
KAJ 109 (see lines 8 f.; cf. page 231, above)
KAJ 114 (see lines 3 ff., 16; cf. page 230, above)
KAJ 119 (see lines 6 f ; cf. page 230, above)
KAJ 121 (see lines 14 f.; cf. page 233, above).

On this basis, it is safe to assign the following tablets to the same reign:

1. *KAJ* 72 (see lines 3 ff.)
2. *KAJ* 73 (see lines 3 ff.)

[52] Note that the name of the scribe of *KAJ* 54, Uṣur-ša-pî-šarri (line 23), may be mentioned in *Assur* 9819, rev 16 If the identification can be established, the reign of Shalmaneser would be the most likely time of origin for this tablet At any rate, the reign of Tukulti-Ninurta is an impossibility (Contrast Weidner, *AfO*, XIII, page 117)

[53] For more precise dating in the reign of Shalmaneser, see below, page 258

[54] For a discussion of the eponymy of Abattu, see pages 245 f , above

[55] It is not possible, with Ebeling (*Eigennamen*, page 83), to identify the witness of *KAJ* 98, 19 f (*Šamaš-kîna-uṣur mâr Adad-šar mâr Šamaš-mâlik*) with the witness of *KAJ* 26, 20 (*Šamaš-kîna-uṣur mâr* [ ]) On the date of *KAJ* 26, see page 207, above)

[56] For Ebeling's dating in the reign of Erîba-Adad (*Urkunden*, page 85), see above, note 51

3. *KAJ* 94 (see lines 2 f.)
4. *KAJ* 95 (see lines 3 ff.)
5. *KAJ* 102 (see line 8)
6. *KAJ* 108 (see lines 3 f.)
7. *KAJ* 118 (see lines 3 f.)
8. *KAJ* 120 (see lines 21 f.)
9. *KAJ* 315 (see line 4).

C. The Date of Urad-Šerua, son of Melisaḫ.

1. The following tablets of Urad-Šerua belong, likewise, in the reign of Shalmaneser:

KAJ 48 (see lines 2 f.; cf. page 236, above)
KAJ 49 (see lines 2 f.; cf page 237, above)
KAJ 80 (see lines 9 f.; cf. page 232, above)
KAJ 109 (see lines 15 f.; cf. page 231, above)
KAJ 113 (see lines 34 f.; cf. page 231, above)
KAJ 115 (see lines 14 f., cf. page 232, above)
KAV 156 (see line 11;[57] cf. page 236, above).[58]

[57] It is possible, here also, that the same Urad-Šerua is involved *KAV* 156 (cf line 10) is contemporary to *KAJ* 124 (cf line rev 6), both documents being written in the eponymy of Aššur-daisunu However, *KAJ* 124 involves a transaction of [B]alṭu-kâšid, the *aškapu* (line 2), who appears also in *KAJ* 223 (line 5) Moreover, *KAJ* 223, (cf line 14) is written in the same year as *KAJ* 48 (cf line 21), namely in the eponymy year of Lulaiau, and *KAJ* 48 involves a transaction of *Urad-Šerua mâr Melisaḫ*, therefore *KAV* 156 is, at any rate, contemporary with the activity of this Urad-Šerua, and the official involved in the transaction may, without too much risk, be identified as the son of Melisaḫ

The possibility of reading Urad-Šerua in line 10 is not suggested in Ebeling's *Eigennamen* (page 19)

[58] The complete list shows that there is little justification for Weidner's assumption that the greater part of the career of Urad-Šerua took place under Tukulti-Ninurta, and that perhaps Mušallim-Aššur served for two terms as *lîmu*, once under Shalmaneser, and once under his successor (*AfO*, XIII, page 114)

Admittedly, it is strange that in this one eponymy year both grandfather (*KAJ* 83), father (*KAJ* 109), and son (*KAJ* 109, 113) were active in their careers Beyond this one tablet, we have no evidence that the career of Urad-Šerua overlapped that of his father, although the careers of Aššur-aḫ-iddina and Melisaḫ were contemporary for a period of years (see the synchronistic tables at the end of this chapter).

However, the fact that Urad-Šerua plays a somewhat different role in

2. The following tablets belong in the reign of Tukulti-Ninurta:

KAJ 110 (see lines 14 f.; cf. page 240, above)
KAJ 111 (cf. above, page 241)[59]
KAJ 116 (see lines rev 8; cf. page 241, above)
KAJ 122 (see lines 12 f.; cf. page 240, above)
KAJ 128 (see lines 5 f.; cf page 241, above).

On this basis, therefore, the following tablets of Urad-Šerua are to be assigned to the reign of Shalmaneser or Tukulti-Ninurta:

1. *KAJ* 112 (?) (see line 11)[60]
2. *KAJ* 245[61] (see line 14)[62]
3. *KAJ* 268 (see line 12).

KAJ 109 and 113 makes it unnecessary to conjecture that Mušallim-Aššur served a double term See above, note 8 for full details

59 Undoubtedly the wife of Urad-Šerua, mentioned in line 3 of this tablet, is the wife of *Urad-Šerua mâr Melisaḫ* The following considerations prove this conclusion:

i) She is the daughter of Ittabši-dên-Aššur A son of Ittabši-dên-Aššur appears together with Urad-Šerua, the son of Melisaḫ, as a *qîpu* of the king (*KAJ* 116, rev. 8 f ; cf *Assur* 9819, and the discussion of this tablet on pages 247 f)

ii) The tablet is written by the same scribe as *KAJ* 128, likewise a tablet of *Urad-Šerua mâr Melisaḫ*

60 Since the *lîmu* of *KAJ* 112 (Šunu-qardu, line 17) is the same as that of *KAJ* 268 (line 16), it is likely that the same Urad-Šerua is intended in this tablet

61 Once again the identification of Urad-Šerua (line 14) with the son of Melisaḫ is tempting In this document, he appears as a powerful official into whose charge certain persons belonging to the king (line 7) and to others are entrusted Moreover, the document is written in the eponymy of Adad-bêl-gabbê (line 20), a *lîmu* known also from *KAV* 102 (line 22) and 105 (line 32) These documents of Bâbu-aḫ-iddina belong at any rate to the general period under discussion, and offer some chronological confirmation of this hypothesis It should be noted that the Adad-bêl-gabbê who gives his name to the year of origin of these tablets is not to be identified with the Adad-bêl-gabbê of *KAJ* 212, 2, a document to be dated in the following century (contrast Ebeling, *Eigennamen*, page 7)

62 This dating of *KAJ* 112 and 245 confirms our conclusion that the officials mentioned in *Assur* 9819 (see above, pages 247 ff) were active in the general period around the reign of Tukulti-Ninurta

D. It may be further assumed that, although overlapping to some extent, the activity of grandfather, father and son were, for the most part, consecutive. Thus, neither Melisaḫ nor Urad-Šerua is known to have been active in the reign of Adad-nirâri; and neither Aššur-aḫ-iddina nor Melisaḫ appears in tablets which might, on any basis, be assigned to the reign of Tukulti-Ninurta.

For this reason it is possible to arrange the eponymy years of these documents in successive groups, of which the eponymy years within each group are, broadly speaking, later than those of the previous group and earlier than those of the succeeding group. A full synchronism of the activity of these men is apparent on the basis of the chronological tables at the conclusion of this chapter.

E. The following tablets, by means of parallels with documents of Aššur-aḫ-iddina, may be dated in the general period of his activity, namely, the reigns of Adad-nirâri and the first years of Shalmaneser:

1. *KAJ* 227 (see line 7)
2. *KAJ* 232 (see line 12)
3. *KAV* 110 (see line 7)
4. *KAV* 111 (see line 9)
5. *KAV* 157 (see line 9)
6. *KAV* 158 (see line 12).

All of the above documents were written in the eponymy of Ninurta-emuqâia, the same year as *KAJ* 76 (see line 28).

F. The following documents belong in the reign of Shalmaneser, and are contemporary with the activity of Melisaḫ:

1. *KAJ* 81. The *lîmu* of this document, Aššur-mušabši (line 29), is likewise the *lîmu* of *KAJ* 108 (line 13); 118 (line 26); and 120 (line 32). An approximation of the date of *KAJ* 81 is given above, page 255.[63]

[63] *KAJ* 56 is not to be more accurately dated on the supposition that the creditor, as well as the debtor, is the same as that of *KAJ* 81 Note the following comparisons·

2 *KAJ* 258(?), 253(?). Perhaps the Samidu of *KAJ* 258, 2 is likewise intended in the fragment *KAJ* 315 (line 5), a document of Melisaḫ.

Both *KAJ* 258 (line 8) and *KAJ* 253 (line 10) were written in the eponymy of Kidin-ilâni (See above, note 10).

G. The following tablets are contemporary with the career of Urad-Šerua, and belong in the period of Shalmaneser/Tukulti-Ninurta:

1. *KAJ* 178 (see line 23); *KAV* 109 (see line 31). The *lîmu* of both of these tablets, Šunu-qardu,[64] is likewise *lîmu* of *KAJ* 112 (line 17) and 268 (line 16).
2. *KAV* 102 (see line 22); 105 (see line 32) The *lîmu* of these tablets, Adad-bêl-gabbe, is also the *lîmu* of *KAJ* 245, 20

PART 4 — THE ACTIVITY OF BÂBU-AḪ-IDDINA

The career of Bâbu-aḫ-iddina has been fully studied by Ebeling.[65] The identification of a few additional documents which deal with his transactions, as well as some notes on chronology are all that need be added here.

A. The following tablets represent the letters or transactions which involved Bâbu-aḫ-iddina or his lieutenants

KAJ 123 (see line 4)
KAJ 125 (see line 4)[66]
KAJ 158 (see line 8)

(*KAJ* 56, 5 f) *i-na muḫḫi* ^{m}*Da[ẓẓân*] (line 6) *mâr* ^{d}*Adad-[*]
(*KAJ* 81, 6 f) *i-na muḫḫi* ^{m}*Adad-aḫ-iddina*^{na} (line 7) *mâr Daẓẓân-i-ẓa*(?)

Ebeling restored both *Dajân[na]* and ^{d}*Adad-[aḫ-iddina]* in *KAJ* 56, identifying each man with his namesake in *KAJ* 81 (*Eigennamen*, pages 6, 36), thereby identifying in at least one instance grandfather and grandson

64 For a discussion with regard to *Assur* 9819, see above, page 248

65 *Urkunden*, pp 5–25

66 This tablet is apparently the basis for Ebeling's suggestion that Ašur-zukupanni (*Eigennamen*, page 29), as well as Ibašši-ilu (*ibid* , pages 30, 43), is the father of Bâbu-aḫ-iddina The probable reading of lines 4 ff , however, is·

(line 4) *ša* ^{md}*Ba-bu-aḫ-iddina*^{na} (line 5) [*ša qâ*]*t* ^{md}*A-šur-zu-kup-pa-ni*
(line 6) [*ša*? *i-na muḫ-ḫi*] ^{md}*A-šur-mu-šab-ši*

KAJ 159 (see line rev. 4)[67]
KAJ 178 (see line 15)
KAJ 217 (if Manaịau, line 5, is the lieutenant of Bâbu-aḫ-iddina; cf. note 67)
KAJ 242 (see line rev. 2)
KAJ 256 (?)[68]
KAJ 274 (see line 7)[69]
KAJ 279 (see line 4)
KAJ 293a[70]
KAJ 306 (?)[71]
KAV 96 (see line 4)
KAV 98 (see line 4)
KAV 99 (see line 4)
KAV 100 (see line 5)
KAV 102 (see line 4)
KAV 103 (see line 6)
KAV 104[72]

[67] The reading *^{d}[Ba-bu]-aḫ-iddina^{na} m[âr] Ibašši-ilu* as the indebted party of this tablet is clear on the basis of the occurrence as witness to the transaction of one of the known lieutenants of Bâbu-aḫ-iddina, namely *Ma'naịau mâr ^{f}Gangiịa* (cf *KAJ* 123, 8 f , etc), and likewise on the basis of the recurrence in this tablet of the same creditors of Bâbu-aḫ-iddina as appear in *KAJ* 158, namely *Kurbanu mâr Siịaêni* (*KAJ* 158, 3, 159, 6) and *Nabû-kittum mâr Murâni* (*KAJ* 158, 5 f ; 159, 7).

[68] See note 72 below

[69] Once again identifying Ma'naịau as the lieutenant of Bâbu-aḫ-iddina. Note also Siqi-ilâni (line 12, cf *KAV* 98, 6; 109, 15)

[70] In this tablet, several of the lieutenants of Bâbu-aḫ-iddina participate.

Aššur-zuqupanni (lines 2, 20, cf *KAJ* 125, 5; *KAV* 99, 2; etc)
Aššur-šallimani (lines 4, 7, 10, 21; cf. *KAV* 99, 5, 106, 3)
Aššur-bêl-šallim (line 8; cf. *KAV* 98, 2, 99, 2; etc)

[71] Perhaps *KAJ* 306, 4 is to be read:

^{md}A-šur-bêl-[šallim],

who is known to be a lieutenant of Bâbu-aḫ-iddina (cf Ebeling, *Eigennamen*, page 22)

[72] Placed in this group on the basis of Mušallim-Aššur (N B line 3; cf *KAV* 98, 5, 99, 5, etc) and of Bâbu-apla-uṣur (lines 4, 21, cf *KAJ* 178, line 19) (Perhaps the same Bâbu-apla-uṣur is intended in *KAJ* 256, 3 If so, this becomes our only means of dating this tablet)

Note also that the *lîmu* of *KAV* 104, 25 (Usât-Marduk) is the same as that of *KAV* 98, 50

KAV 105 (see line 4)
KAV 106 (see line 4)
KAV 107 (see line 4)
KAV 108[73]
KAV 109 (see line 4)
KAV 194 (see line 3)
KAV 196 (see line 3)
KAV 200 (see line 4)
KAV 203 (see line 6)
KAV 205 (see line 5).

B. The Date of Bâbu-aḫ-iddina.[74]

1. The following tablets in which Bâbu-aḫ-iddina or his lieutenants participate may be dated in the reign of Adad-nirâri:

KAV 96 (see above, page 228)
KAV 107 (see above, page 228)
KAV 194 (see above, page 228).

2. The following tablets have been assigned to the reign of Shalmaneser:

KAJ 123 (see above, page 231)
KAJ 125 (see above, page 236)
KAJ 158 (see above, page 232)
KAJ 159 (see above, page 232)
KAJ 217 (see above, page 236)
KAJ 242 (see above, page 230)
KAV 98 (see above, page 236)

[73] Note the following lieutenants of Bâbu-aḫ-iddina.
Aššur-zu[qupanni] (line 1, cf note 63)
Mušallim-^{d}[Aššur] (line 3; cf. *KAV* 98, 5, 99, 5, etc).

[74] There is no possibility of maintaining, with Koschaker, that the career of Bâbu-aḫ-iddina began in the reign of Aššur-uballit (*NRU*, page 8, note 1) The Eribtaiau who is *lîmu* of *KAJ* 159 cannot be the participant in the contract of *KAJ* 10, among other reasons, because the father of each of the two men is different (*KAJ* 10, 14, cf 11 f, gives the father of Eribtaiau as Kurbanu The father of the *lîmu* of *KAJ* 159 is Abi-ilu). Thus *KAJ* 159, a Bâbu-aḫ-iddina tablet, cannot be dated on the basis of *KAJ* 10, in the reign of Aššur-uballiṭ

KAV 103 (see above, page 232)
KAV 104 (see above, page 236)
KAV 203 (see above, page 232).

3 The following documents belong either to the reign of Shalmaneser or to that of Tukulti-Ninurta:

KAJ 178 (see above, page 259)
KAV 102 (see above, page 259)
KAV 105 (see above, page 259)[75]
KAV 109 (see above, page 259)

4 The following documents belong to the last year of the reign of Shalmaneser.

KAV 106 (see above, page 240)
KAV 200 (see above, page 240).

5. The following document belongs to the first regnal year of Tukulti-Ninurta·

KAV 196 (see above, page 240).

Thus, the career of Bâbu-aḫ-iddina is known to have been in progress in the reign of Adad-nirâri, and to have continued at least into the first years of the reign of Tukulti-Ninurta It may, of course, have lasted some years beyond these limits in either direction.

C. A few of the remaining documents can be dated somewhat more precisely than these remarks would at first indicate.

[75] There is not sufficient evidence to make a positive identification of the *Tâb-ṣilli-Aššur* of *KAV* 105, 9, with the *Tâb-ṣilli-Aššur mâr Aššur-multêpiš*, who is the second witness of *KAJ* 54 (lines 19 f), thereby dating the Bâbu-aḫ-iddina tablet (*KAV* 105) in the reign of Adad-nirâri or Shalmaneser

It is true that *Ṭâb-ṣilli-Aššur* seems to be the correct reading, despite the identification of the witness' seal in line 30, where the name is given as *Ṭâb-ṣilli-Šamaš* As far as can be made out, Ebeling indicates that the name in line 19 is written over an erasure, which points to the fact that here, also, the scribe had written *Tâb-ṣilli-Šamaš*, which he later corrected, neglecting to make the same correction in line 30

Nevertheless, the mere occurrence of a single name without patronymic or other identification, cannot give us a positive identification in this case, nor a means of finding more than a general date for the tablet in question.

1. *KAJ* 293a and *KAV* 99. It appears that Aššur-šallimani (*KAJ* 293a, 4, *KAV* 99, 5) joined the service of Bâbu-aḫ-iddina only in the later years of his activity. At any rate, the only other document mentioning him is *KAV* 106 (line 3), which belongs to the last regnal year of Shalmaneser. It may also be significant that Ešir-dên-Nusku (*KAV* 99, 7) appears elsewhere in these tablets only in *KAV* 203, 8, a document of the reign of Shalmaneser.

It should be noted, moreover, that the *lîmu*-officer of *KAV* 99, Ittabši-dên-Aššur, is one of the officials listed in the document *Assur* 9819. A date in the reigns of Shalmaneser or Tukulti-Ninurta therefore seems probable on this basis also.

Thus, there can be no objection to limiting the date of origin of these tablets to the reigns of Shalmaneser or Tukulti-Ninurta.

2. *KAJ* 279 (see line 12) and *KAV* 205 (see line 39), which have the same *lîmu*, Ittabši-dên-Aššur, as *KAV* 99 (line 47), may be set in the period of the same two reigns.[76]

D. The remaining tablets are to be assigned, quite generally, to the widest known range of the activity of Bâbu-aḫ-iddina, between the reigns of Adad-nirâri and Tukulti-Ninurta:

KAJ 256
KAJ 274
KAJ 306
KAV 100
KAV 108

E. The following tablet may be contemporary to some of the documents of Bâbu-aḫ-iddina which have been supposed to originate in the period of the reigns of Shalmaneser and Tukulti-Ninurta:

1. *KAV* 217(?). Is the *Taklak-ana-A*[*ššur*] of line 21 the same as the person mentioned in *KAJ* 279, 7? If so, then [*Mu*]*šallim-Adad*, who appears in *KAV* 217, 20, may be the *lîmu* of the third year of Tukulti-Ninurta (*KAJ* 240, 26).

[76] It is difficult to understand why Ebeling (*Eigennamen*, page 51) does not identify the *lîmu* of *KAJ* 279 with that of the remaining two tablets

F. The following tablet is to be dated at some time between the reigns of Adad-nirâri and Tukulti-Ninurta on the basis of parallels with *KAJ* 274:

KAJ 190. The *lîmu* of this tablet, Ana-pî-Aššur-lišlim (line 25), is doubtless the same as that of *KAJ* 274, 4, 18, Ina-pî-Aššur-lišlim.[77]

[77] Ebeling appears uncertain as to the correct reading of *KAJ* 274, 18. The spelling of the *lîmu* of this document is given as follows:

(line 4) *ša i-na li-me* ^{m} 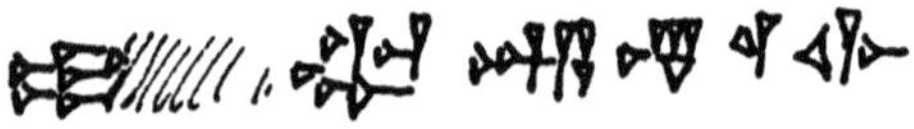

(cf., line 18) ^{m} 

But Ebeling reads it once in accordance with a hypothetical reconstruction of *KAJ* 230, 14:

[I-na]-qi-bi-^{d}*A-šur-[liš-lim]* (*Eigennamen*, page 48);

and once in accordance with *KAJ* 190, 25:

A(*sic!*)*-na-pî-*^{d}*A-šur-liš-lim* (*ibid.*, page 16)

Although an emendation is not justified, however, it is possible that the same *lîmu* is referred to in both cases, and is to be read:

Ana(*Ina*)*-pî-Aššur-lišlim*

The *lîmu* of *KAJ* 230 is known from other documents as Qibi-Aššur (see above, page 240)

TABLE V

Documents and Eponymies of the Thirteenth Century

Group 1a) The Reign of Adad-nirâri

Lîmu	Tablets Involving Aššur-aḫ-iddina	Tablets Involving Melisaḫ	Tablets Involving Urad-Šerua	Other Tablets
Kurbânu				*KAJ* 10 *Bi* 91
Ša-Adad-nînu	*KAJ* 145			*Bi* 15 *Bi* 40
Šulmânu-qarrâd				*KAJ* 307
Aššur-eriš				*KAV* 96 *KAV* 107 *KAV* 194

Group 1b) The Reigns of Adad-nirâri-Shalmaneser

Activity of Aššur-aḫ-iddina

Lîmu	Tablets Involving Aššur-aḫ-iddina	Tablets Involving Melisaḫ	Tablets Involving Urad-Šerua	Other Tablets
Rîš-Aššur	*KAJ* 54			
Adad-šamši	*KAJ* 56			
Šulmânu-qarrâd	*KAJ* 75 (but see *Sulmânu-ašarid*)			
Ninurta-emuqâia	*KAJ* 76			*KAJ* 227 *KAJ* 232 *KAV* 110 *KAV* 111 *KAV* 157 *KAV* 158
Aššur-mušêzib	*KAJ* 98			
Aššur-mudammiq	*KAJ* 130			
Agi-Tešup	*KAJ* 137			
Aššur-sadû-nišêsu				*CT* 33,14b *Bi* 38
Unstated	*KAJ* 100			

Group 1c) The Reign of Shalmaneser

Activity of Aššur-aḫ-iddina

Lîmu	Tablets Involving Aššur-aḫ-iddina	Tablets Involving Melisaḫ	Tablets Involving Urad-Šerua	Other Tablets
Šulmânu-ašarid	*KAJ* 75 (but see *Šulmânu-qarrâd*)			*Bi* 13
Abattu mâr Adad-šumu-lîšir	*KAJ* 89			*KAJ* 316 (?)
Aššur-dammiq	*KAJ* 262			*KAJ* 123

Group 2a) The Reign of Shalmaneser
Joint Activity of Aššur-aḫ-iddina and Melisaḫ

Abi-ılı ↓		*KAJ* 119		*KAJ* 242 *KAJ* 290
Aššur-âlık-pâni ↓	*KAJ* 62	*KAJ* 114		
Mušallim-Aššur	*KAJ* 83	*KAJ* 109	*KAJ* 109[78] *KAJ* 113	
Aššur-mušabši	*KAJ* 81	*KAJ* 108 *KAJ* 118 *KAJ* 120		
Kidın-Sîn mâr Adadteja				*Bı* 9[79]
Aššur-bêl-ılâni				*KAJ* 171[80]
Ber-šum-lîšır				*Speleers* No. 314[81]
Unstated				*KAJ* 275(?)[82]

[78] See above, notes 8 and 58 for a discussion of these tablets of Urad-Šerua which belong to a period before the beginning of his general activity

[79] Placed in this group on the basis of the parallel with *KAJ* 109 See page 235 above

[80] Placed in this group on the basis of the parallel with *KAJ* 114

[81] Placed in this group on the basis of the parallel with *KAJ* 113

[82] Placed in this group on the basis of the parallel with *KAJ* 109

Group 2b) The Reign of Shalmaneser

Activity of Melisaḫ

Lîmu	Tablets Involving Aššur-aḫ-iddina	Tablets Involving Melisaḫ	Tablets Involving Urad-Šerua	Other Tablets
Aššur-kâšid		*KAJ* 51 *KAJ* 90		*Bi* 8
Putanu		*KAJ* 72		
Ilu-qarrâd		*KAJ* 73		
Ber-šum-iddina		*KAJ* 94 *KAJ* 102		
Kidin-ilâni (?)[83]				*KAJ* 253 (?) *KAJ* 258 (?)
Unstated		*KAJ* 95 *KAJ* 121 *KAJ* 315		

[83] Dated in this group on the basis of the parallel to *KAJ* 51.

Group 3a) The Reign of Shalmaneser
Activity of Urad-Šerua

Lîmu	Tablets Involving Aššur-aḫ-iddina	Tablets Involving Melisaḫ	Tablets Involving Urad-Šerua	Other Tablets
Šamaš-Kitti-idi			*KAJ* 49	*KAJ* 59 (?)
Ištar-eriš ↓				*KAJ* 124a *KAJ* 219 *KAV* 119 *Bi* 25 *Bi* 31
Aššur-da'isunu			*KAV* 156	*KAJ* 124
↓ *Usât-Marduk*				*KAJ* 104 *KAJ* 125 *KAV* 98 *KAV* 104
Eribtaiau ↓				*KAJ* 159 *KAJ* 267 *Bi* 5
Enlil-ašarid			*KAJ* 80 *KAJ* 115	*KAJ* 308 *KAJ* 311 *KAV* 103 *KAV* 203
Aššur-kitti-idi[84]				*KAJ* 182 *KAJ* 184 *KAJ* 225
Ber-bêl-litte (*Ber-bêl-la-itte*)				*KAJ* 217 *KAJ* 314
↓ *Lulaiau*			*KAJ* 48	*KAJ* 223 *KAJ* 310
Unstated				*KAJ* 158[85]

[84] Placed in this group on the basis of *KAJ* 267

[85] Placed in this group on the basis of *KAJ* 159

Group 3b) Reigns of Shalmaneser/Tukultı-Ninurta
Activity of Urad-Šerua

Lîmu	Tablets Involving Aššur-aḫ-iddına	Tablets Involving Melısaḫ	Tablets Involving Urad-Šerua	Other Tablets
Lıbur-zânın-Aššur				KAJ 88 KAJ 168 KAJ 218 KAJ 318
Nabû-bêl-uṣur				KAJ 97
Šunu-qardu			KAJ 112 KAJ 268	KAJ 178 KAV 109
Adad-bêl-gabbe			KAJ 245	KAV 102 KAV 105
Ittabšı-dên-Aššur				KAJ 279 KAV 99 KAV 205
Unstated				KAJ 15 KAJ 93 KAJ 127 KAJ 228 KAJ 263 KAJ 271 KAJ 292 KAJ 293 KAJ 293a KAJ 313 KAV 201 KAV 217 (?)

Group 3c) The Reign of Tukulti-Ninurta
(Including the last year of Shalmaneser)
Activity of Urad-Šerua

Līmu	Tablets Involving Aššur-aḫ-iddina	Tablets Involving Melisaḫ	Tablets Involving Urad-Šerua	Other Tablets
Upru ↓				KAJ 180 KAV 106 KAV 200
Tukultı-Ninurta ↓				KAJ 138 KAJ 144 KAJ 238 KAJ 272 KAJ 312 KAV 196
Qıbi-Aššur ↓				KAJ 230 KAJ 289 KAJ 291
Mušallım-Adad			KAJ 122	KAJ 110 KAJ 240 KAJ 241 KAJ 244
Abattu mār Adad-šamši ↓				KAJ 30 KAJ 316 (?) KAV 201 (?)[86]
Etıl-pî-Aššur				KAJ 301

[86] See note 35, above.

Lîmu	Tablets Involving Aššur-aḫ-iddina	Tablets Involving Melisaḫ	Tablets Involving Urad-Šerua	Other Tablets
Aššur-zêr-iddina				*KAJ* 103 *KAJ* 106
Enlil-nâdin-apli				*KAJ* 107 (=117) *KAJ* 133 *KAJ* 319
Aššur-dân-mâr Ikkari			*KAJ* 111	*KAV* 168
Ilu-šu-mušallim			*KAJ* 116	
Aššur-nâdin-apli			*KAJ* 128	*KAV* 169
Sarniqu				*KAJ* 255

Group X

Tablets belonging to this general period
(Adad-nirâri to Tukulti-Ninurta),
but not more precisely dateable

Lîmu	Tablets
Ina-pî-Aššur-lišlim (=*Ana-pî-Aššur-lišlim*?)	*KAJ 274* *KAJ* 190 (?)
Unstated	*KAJ* 256 *KAJ* 306 (?) *KAV* 100 *KAV* 108

Part II

CHAPTER IV

The Rule of Ninurta-tukulti-Aššur

I. Among the most thoroughly documented years within the Middle-Assyrian period is the eponymy year of Sîn-šei̯a. Starting in the month before his accession to the eponymy,[1] each month of the twelve-month period is represented by at least one,[2] and generally by several official documents and memoranda concerning tribute and offerings presented to Ninurta-tukulti-Aššur. The tablets have been studied in detail by Ebeling and by Weidner,[3] from whose conclusions much of the following material is summarized.

The tablets were originally assumed to come from the reign of Ninurta-tukulti-Aššur,[4] who plays a prominent role in more

[1] The immediate succession of the two eponymy years of Aššur-šêzibanni and Sîn-šei̯a is demonstrated in *W.* 50, where lines 40–44 are transliterated by Weidner as follows·

iš-tu araḫ ḫi-bur ûmu 11$^{ka[n}$ *l]i-me*
^{m}*Aš-šur-êṭir-a-ni mâr Pa-'u-z[i]*
a-di araḫ ṣi-pi ûmu 28^{kan}
li-me ^{md}*Sin-še-i̯a*
mâr Arad-ilâni^{meš}

[2] On the month of *muḫur-ilâni*, see *Assur* 13058, 13 transliterated by Weidner, *AfO* X, page 30

[3] Ebeling, *Urkunden*, pages 26–37, Weidner, "Aus den Tagen eines assyrischen Schattenkonigs," *AfO* X, pages 1–52 Beyond the texts published in *KAJ*, and listed below, Ebeling presents, in the *Urkunden*, three further documents from this period (*VAT* 9363, 9378, 9405) Weidner, in addition to these, gives in his article the transliteration of two historical texts (*Assur* 12758, 13058, pages 30 ff) and of numerous memoranda, etc , which are parallel to the tablets published in *KAJ*, and which he numbers from 50 to distinguish them from Ebeling's publications (*W* 50–111, *op cit*)

[4] *Ibid*

than half of the transactions. With the discovery of the Khorsabad King List, however, some doubts have arisen concerning this conclusion. Poebel[5] finds the following objections to Weidner's theory of the "Schattenkonig":

1) the title "king" is never given to Ninurta-tukulti-Aššur in the entire collection of documents;

2) the tablets cover a period of almost twelve months, a possibility quite precluded in Poebel's chronological interpretation of the King List;[6] and finally,

3) the mention of the "100 sheep of Mutakkil-Nusku" (*W.* 98) brings Poebel to reject Weidner's theory that Ninurta-tukulti-Aššur was a usurper to the throne,[7] and hence his entire chronological reconstruction.

On the other hand, by contesting Poebel's understanding of the term *ṭuppišu*,[8] as used in the King List, Weidner attempts to maintain his former conclusion that the documents in question belong to the actual reign of Ninurta-tukulti-Aššur.[9] Weidner

[5] *JNES* II, pages 62 ff.

[6] "The year in which Ninurta-tukulti-Aššur was king also comprised, as we now know, a fraction of the reign of Aššur-dân, as well as the reign of Mutakkil-Nusku and a fraction of the reign of Aššur-rêša-iši," *ibid* page 65 Poebel relies upon the explanation of "*ṭuppišu*" given by Oppenheim, *RA* XXXIII, pages 143 ff.

[7] This last objection, however, is hardly decisive in a discussion of the chronological problem The Khorsabad King List makes it evident that Weidner can no longer maintain the hypothesis of Ninurta-tukulti-Aššur's usurpation (cf. *AfO* XIV, page 366) But this should not affect any conclusion concerning the length of his reign. Moreover, the role of Mutakkil-Nusku in this tablet is not the same as that of Ninurta-tukulti-Aššur in the contemporary documents The memorandum says nothing of a *namurtu* which is offered to him It is therefore not "quite obvious," on this basis at least, that "the tablets mentioning Ninurta-tukulti-Aššur and Mutakkil-Nusku date from the time of Aššur-dân, in which both brothers had no higher rank than that of royal princes" (*loc cit.*). Even if Ninurta-tukulti-Aššur is only crown-prince at the time of these documents, his status as the receiver of *namurâte* is at any rate superior to that of his brother.

[8] In the King List, Rev. I, lines 32–36.
^{Id}Ninurta-tukul-ti-aš-šur / mâr ^{I}aš-šur-dân^{a}[^{n}] (line 33) *ṭup-pi-šú / šarru-ta êpuš^{uš}* (line 34) *^{I}mu-tak-kil-^{d}nusku / aḫu-šú itti-šú i-duk .* (line 36) *ṭup-pi-šú ^{I}mu-tak-kil-^{d}nusku ^{is}kussâ / uk-ta-il šadâ^{a} e-mid* (transliteration of Weidner, *AfO* XIV, page 364)

[9] *Ibid* , page 366, cf. *AfO* XIII, page 111, note 12

will not admit that the term is employed to designate the reign of a king who does not enjoy a full regnal year On the contrary, he takes the usage in the Khorsabad King List as proof that the term is used to designate the reign of a king which extends precisely for one year.

Weidner's conclusion is modified by Landsberger.[10] On the basis of parallel usages, Landsberger attempts to show that *ṭuppišu* is a term used to designate any unspecified period of time.[11] Hence, he concludes, there is no difficulty in maintaining Weidner's conclusion that all of the tablets come from the reign of Ninurta-tukulti-Aššur, the duration of which is not to be determined.

It seems unlikely, however, in view of the precise formulation of the Khorsabad King List, that two brief periods of time should have been totally unaccounted for by the Assyrian chroniclers, and that they should have been so vague concerning the length of the reigns of the six successors of Aššur-dugul (Col 2, lines 10 f.) or of the two sons of Aššur-dân (Col. rev. 1, lines 33, 36). According to Landsberger, it is tendencious reasoning to expect exactness and continuity in such a historical source, and to interpret it in agreement with such expectation.[12] Actually, however, the King List gives the unmistakable impression of attempting such accuracy; and Landsberger himself is forced to assume that, in the second case at any rate, a sense of shame at the strife of the two royal brothers led the chroniclers to suppress the length of their reign.[13]

Furthermore, Landsberger's criticisms of Poebel's translations, although justified in some details, do not disprove the main conclusion which Poebel sought to draw from the use of the expression *ṭuppišu*, as it is found in the King List. If *ṭuppišu* cannot be considered as an abbreviation of *ina ṭuppišu*,[14] it might still be read, in the sense intended by Poebel, as an accusative of time Poebel's theory of textual corruption[15] is, of course, unsatisfactory. But Landsberger's solution, the trans-

[10] "Jahreszeiten im Sumerisch-Akkadischen," *JNES* VIII, pages 265 ff

[11] Thus, the difficulty presented by Column II, lines 10 f of the King List (*6 šarrâni bâb ṭuppišu šarrûta êpuš*) would be obviated *Ibid*, pages 267, 270

[12] *Op. cit*, page 268.

[13] *Ibid*, page 269.

[14] See *ibid.*, page 268.

[15] *JNES* I, page 462

lation of *6 šarrâni* by "eine Sechszahl von Konigen,"[16] in no way eliminates Poebel's chronological hypothesis, and should not, therefore, be urged as a criticism of Poebel's conclusion. Nor is Poebel's interpretation of *ukta'il* as a pluperfect[17] absolutely necessary to his thesis.

Landsberger's criticisms of Poebel are not, therefore, definitive in the interpretation of the King List. Even if Landsberger's explanation of *ṭuppu* as an unspecified period of time is correct, such a meaning may, for the King List, be reconciled with Poebel's chronological reconstruction. Assuming, with Poebel, that the suffix *–šu*, as used with the term *ṭuppu* in the King List, has reference, always, to the preceding king, then "his period" could, without difficulty, have come to mean "the unexpired period of his last regnal year."

The only problem, therefore, is to reconcile the chronology of the King List with the fact that the juridical tablets in question must, by any system of reckoning, extend for at least one full year.[18] The long reign which is assigned to Aššur-dân, the father of Ninurta-tukulti-Aššur, suggests the possibility of a solution.[19] It is not unreasonable to suppose that towards the end of his father's reign, Ninurta-tukulti-Aššur acted as regent of the kingdom. In this way, we may explain the importance which he assumes in these memoranda, and the vast quantity

[16] *Op. cit*, page 267

[17] *JNES* II, page 70

[18] The Assyrian year at this time began in the month of *Sippu*, whereas the tablets in question extend from the first day of *Ḫibur*, the twelfth month of the preceding year, until *Abu-šarrâni*, the eleventh month of the eponymy of Sîn-šeja Thus, whether by a system of post-dating or of ante-dating, at least one of these two years would have to be reckoned to the reign of Ninurta-tukulti-Aššur if he were king during the period of the writing of the tablets On the beginning of the Assyrian year with the month of *Sippu*, see the references to *KAJ* 10 and *Assur* 13058kl in Lewy, *AC*, page 35 Lewy has also called my attention to *KAJ* 106, where the *ûm šarri* (line 12) seems to be the first day of *Sippu* (line 18). Since the eponymy year in this period likewise begins in *Ṣippu*, the confusion of the calendar which is observed in late Middle-Assyrian times must have become evident only after the reign of Ninurta-tukulti-Aššur On this calendric confusion, see Weidner, *AfO* V, page 184; X, pages 28 f , Lewy, "The Assyrian Calendar," *AO* XI, p 46

[19] Weidner, *AfO* XIV, page 364, col. rev I, 31.

of the tribute which is brought to him; and conversely, the absence of the term *uklum* following his name becomes readily understandable.

II. The Documents of this period.

A. The following documents come from the month of *Ḫıbur* in the eponymy of Aššur-šêzıbanni:

KAJ 197	(*Ḫıbur* 28, see lines 1 ff.)
KAJ 237	(*Ḫıbur* 19, see lines 13 f.)
KAJ 281	(*Ḫıbur* 24, see lines 10 f.)
W 51	(*Ḫıbur* 1, see lines 7 f.)
W. 52	(*Ḫıbur* 13, see lines 12 f.)
W. 53	(*Ḫıbur* 19, see lines 10 f.)
W. 54	(*Ḫıbur* 25, see lines 7 f.).

The close connection of his eponymy with that of Sîn-šeia is clear for several reasons, in addition to the indication given by *W*. 50, 40–44·

1) the mention of Ninurta-tukulti-Aššur (*W*. 50, 13; 53, 3.)
2) the mention of *Mutta*, known as an official of Ninurta-tukulti-Aššur from such tablets as *W*. 53 (lines 3, 5) and *KAJ* 282 (lines 5, 7). (See *KAJ* 237, 10; *W*. 51, 4; 52, 6; 53, 5.)
3) the mention of *Buza*, likewise an official of this period, as is shown by *W*. 50 (lines 3, 13) and numerous documents of the eponymy of Sîn-šeia. (See *KAJ* 281, 7; *W*. 50, 3.)

B. The following documents come from the eponymy of Sîn-šeia·

KAJ 131	(*Qarrâtu* 20, see lines 12 ff.)
KAJ 185	(*Allanâtu* 6, see lines 16 f.)
KAJ 186	(*Ṣıppu* 19, see lines 10 ff.)
KAJ 187	(*Sîn* 1, see lines 18 ff.)
KAJ 188	(*Qarrâtu* 29, see lines 18 ff.)
KAJ 189	(*Ṣıppu* 23, see lines 14 f.)
KAJ 191	(*Ša-kınâte* 7, see lines 17 f.)
KAJ 192	(*Tanmartu* 15, see lines 28 f.)
KAJ 193	(*Sîn* 6, see lines 12 f.)

KAJ 194	(*Tanmartu* 25, see lines 8 ff.)
KAJ 195	(*Ša-kınâte* 18, see lines 11 ff.)
KAJ 198	(*Ša-kınâte* 22, see lines 11 ff.)
KAJ 199	(*Ṣıppu* 12, see lines 14 f.)
KAJ 200	(*Kuzallu* 5, see lines 8 ff.)
KAJ 201	(*Qarrâtu* 20, see lines 10 ff.)
KAJ 202	(*Ša-kınâte* 4, see lines 7 ff.)
KAJ 203	(*Ṣıppu* 2, see lines 15 f.)
KAJ 204	(*Qarrâtu* 2, see lines 15 f.)
KAJ 205	(*Ṣıppu* 3, see lines 16 f)
KAJ 206	(*Tanmartu* 7, see lines 10 ff.)
KAJ 207	(*Sîn* 4, see lines 6 ff.)
KAJ 208	(*Ša-kınâte* 15, see lines 19 f.)
KAJ 209	(*Tanmartu* 14?, see lines 1, 14 f.)
KAJ 210	(*Kuzallu* 11, see lines 13 f.)
KAJ 211	(*Allanâtu* 21, see lines 15 ff.)
KAJ 212	(*Allanâtu*, see lines 14 f.)
KAJ 213	(*Allanâtu* 26, see lines 15 ff.)
KAJ 214	(*Sîn* 5, see line 24)[20]
KAJ 216	(*Qarrâtu* 11, see lınes 15 f.)
KAJ 221	(*Qarrâtu* 15, see lınes 12 f.)
KAJ 222[21]	
KAJ 235	(*Qarrâtu*, see lines 7 f.)
KAJ 254	(*Qarrâtu* 18, see lines 22 f.)
KAJ 264	(*Qarrâtu* 21, see lines 19 f.)
KAJ 265	(*Ṣıppu* 16, see lines 12 f.)
KAJ 278	(*Tanmartu* 8, see lınes 12 ff.)
KAJ 280	(*Bêlat-êkallım* 11, see lines 15 ff.)
KAJ 282	(*Allanâtu* 3, see lines 15 f.)
KAJ 283	(*Qarrâtu* 28, see lines 15 f.)

[20] The name of the *lîmu* is restored on the basıs of the mention of Nınurta-tukultı-Aššur (lıne 4), and the month of *Sîn*, whıch excludes the possıbilıty of the eponymy of Aššur-šêzıbannı

[21] Although undated, thıs document ıs evidently from this same period Šamaš-amranni, mentıoned in the tablet among a lıst of mıllers (line 3) and brewers (line 4), ıs undoubtedly the brewer of *KAJ* 213, 8, 214, 17; etc Saggilu (lıne 2) is lıkewise a brewer, known from *KAJ* 214, 15 Urad-Adad the mıller (lıne 3) occurs in *KAJ* 214, 11, 237, 3, and *W* 78, 7

KAJ 284 (*Kuzallu* 17, see lines 10 f.)
KAJ 286 (*Tanmartu* 30, see lines 9 f.)[22]
KAJ 288 (*Qarrâtu* 29, see lines 15 ff.).

In addition to these documents, *W*. 50 and *W*. 55–111 were written in the same year, although the precise date of *W*. 100–111 is not given, and one or two of them may belong to the last month of the eponymy of Aššur-šêzibanni. To these documents are to be added

Assur 13058 (*Muḫur-ilâni* 1), and
Assur 12758

given by Weidner, *AfO*, X, page 30; as well as the documents

VAT 9363 (*Kuzallu*),
VAT 9378 (*Ša-sarrate* 2), and
VAT 9405 (*Qarrâtu* 22)

published by Ebeling (*Urkunden*, page 37). Of these, all except *Assur* 12758 are explicitly from the eponymy of Sîn-šeia; this last tablet is to be dated in the same or in the previous eponymy.

C. It is possible that certain other tablets, not directly contemporary, may be fairly close in time of origin to these documents of the reign of Ninurta-tukulti-Aššur. It should be pointed out, however, that none of the identifications made below can be regarded as definitely established.

1. *KAJ* 92. The following parallels should be noted:

a) Urad-Kube (lines 2 f.) presents fifteen sheep for a feast[23] of the city of Ninua. Perhaps he is to be identified with the *ḫaziânu* of *KAJ* 265 (lines 3 f.) who presents ten sheep to Ninurta-tukulti-Aššur.

[22] The restoration of the name of Sîn-šeia seems reasonable. The form of the document, describing the daily assignment of sheep for the young lions, is characteristic Once again, the month Tanmartu excludes the possibility of the eponymy of Aššur-šêzibanni.

[23] On this interpretation of *ta-kúl-te* (l 4), cf note 25, below.

b) Eru-apla-iddina, a somewhat unusual name, is given as the *līmu* of this tablet (line 12). Can this also be the man who offers a tribute of sheep to Ninurta-tukulti-Aššur (*KAJ* 211, 4)?[24]

2. *KAJ* 101. It is barely possible that the Ninuaja mentioned in this tablet (line 10) is to be identified with the *mušalšiānu* of *KAJ* 92. In *KAJ* 92, he receives fifteen sheep from a certain Urad-Kube for the feeding of Nineveh. In *KAJ* 101, his agent (*Aššur-apıl-ıddina . . . ša dunnı ša ᵐNınuaja Purudaja*, lines 9 ff.) receives a large quantity of grain, ewes, and harvesting men from Adad-ušammiḫ, the *abarakku* of the royal city. Of this grain, the following report is given:

(line 11) . . . *še'um*ᵘᵐ ᵐᵉˢ (line 12) *an-nı-ú i-na la-a šu-a-te* (line 13) *bît-su ú-ba-lı-ṭi*.
["This grain, of that not belonging to him, has kept alive his house"(?)].

In *KAJ* 92, also, a Ninuajâu (lines 7, 9) receives a number of sheep offered by Urad-Kube, and is referred to as the "host" (*mu-šal-šı-a-nu*, line 10).[25] It is possible that the same situation is referred to in both tablets; but such an identification must remain extremely hypothetical.

3. *KAJ* 129.

a) Samnuḫa-ašarid (line 5), the *abarakku* who engages Ninuajâu on behalf of the palace, may be mentioned as one

---

[24] On the other hand, the Ninuajâu who, in this tablet, receives the sheep from Urad-Kube, cannot reasonably be identified with the brewer (ᵃᵐᵉˡRIQ), known from several tablets of the time of Ninurta-tukultı-Aššur (*KAJ* 185, 2 f , 213, 6, 214, 19, 264, 15; 282, 11; *W* 78, 6; 101, 13). The name Nınuajâu seems to be quite common, especially in the later Mıddle-Assyrıan period. In addıtıon to the Ninuajâu of *KAJ* 92 and 101, and to the brewer of the time of Nınurta-tukultı-Aššur, a further Ninuajâu is mentioned in *KAJ* 129 (see below s v *KAJ* 129); and yet another Ninuajâu appears as a *līmu*-officer from the time of Tukultı-Ninurta (*VAT* 16381; see Weidner, *AfO* XIII, Plate VI, line 2)

[25] Interpretation suggested by J. Lewy, from the root *šasû*, "to call" (*HWB*, 676, *Muss-Arnolt*, page 1076) The *ta-kúl-te* of lıne 4 is interpreted as "feast "

of those bringing tribute to Ninurta-tukulti-Aššur in *KAJ* 205, 1.

b) the *lîmu* of this tablet, *Ta-[ḫu-l]u* (line 19, to be restored on the basis of *KAJ* 126, rev. 6; cf Weidner, *AfO* XIII, page 118) may likewise be the tributary of Ninurta-tukulti-Aššur mentioned in *KAJ* 282, 4.[26]

4. *KAJ* 126. This document has the same *lîmu*, Taḫulu, as *KAJ* 129 (see item 3b), above.

5. *KAV* 159. Samnuḫa-ašarid, the official of *KAJ* 205, 1 and *KAJ* 129, 5, may be the *lîmu* intended in *KAV* 159, 12.

6. *KAJ* 302. Ḫimsateja, mentioned as a shipowner in *KAJ* 302, 10, may be the same as *Ḫimsateja mâr Subunija* of *KAV* 159, 2. This possible reading of *KAJ* 302, 10 is overlooked by Ebeling (*Eigennamen*, page 42).

7. *KAJ* 259. Perhaps Ninurtaja, known from *KAJ* 192, 2[27] and from *KAJ* 284, 3 as a *bêl paḫite* of the time of Ninurta-tukulti-Aššur, may be intended likewise in *KAJ* 259, 5, 8.

[26] However, the Ninuajâu of this tablet appears to be a craftsman employed to perform work on the copper implements mentioned in lines 1 and 2 He would hardly be the brewer known from other tablets of the reign of Ninurta-tukulti-Aššur (see above, note 24)

The mention of ^{âl}*Kâr-Tukulti-Ninurta* makes the document not earlier than the reign of Tukulti-Ninurta I Our tentative date, more than a century later, however, is not made impossible by this consideration (but see Weidner, *AfO* XIII, page 118) To be sure, the city of Kâr-Tukulti-Ninurta is mentioned in a text which has been dated by Muller in the reign of a close successor of Tukulti-Ninurta (*Ass. Rit*, Text I, col III, lines 40 ff ; and *ibid*, page 5) But Muller's dating of this text is also based on the assumption that the city was destroyed soon after the death of its founder, linguistic and other evidence permits only a much vaguer approximation of the date of the text

[27] Reading ^{d}*NIN.IB*(!)-*ja* in *KAJ* 192, 2

CHAPTER V

Some Aspects of Assyrian Religion

A chronological arrangement of the onomastic material of the Middle-Assyrian contracts enables us to draw a number of conclusions. The rise and fall in influence of different members of the pantheon[1] reflect, above all, a growing cosmopolitanism, which accompanied the expansion of the Assyrian empire in the thirteenth century. A summary of the relevent information is given in the following tables·

TABLE VI

The Frequency of the Theophorous Elements in Middle-Assyrian Names[2]

I. The fifteenth and fourteenth centuries

Element	Minimum Number of occurrences	Maximum Number of occurrences	Percentage
Adad	31	43	9.6
Amurru	6	7	1.6
Anum	3	3	0 7

[1] Evidently, every numerical difference is not of significance Names which occur only once or twice in a certain period may be lacking elsewhere purely as a result of coincidence. Each of the deities Urra, Išum, and Ḫamru is known in the fourteenth century from one name only; whereas in the documents of the thirteenth century, they are entirely lacking On the other hand, the situation with respect to the deities Ḫarbe, IB and Mer is precisely the reverse Of course, no conclusions are to be drawn from such limited evidence

[2] The conclusions may be checked by using the list of proper names collected by Ebeling (*Eigennamen*), together with the corrections given in the Appendix, pages 135 ff , below The names are to be dated on the basis of the chronological tables which conclude each of the previous chapters The minimum number of references to any person is determined by assuming that' unless otherwise evident on the basis of paternity, profession, etc , the same name may refer to a person already counted in a contemporary document The maximum number is determined by making only the necessary or probable identifications. Since this latter figure is generally the most reliable, it alone has been converted to a percentage The minimum figure is retained to show the largest possible extent of error

TABLE VI (*Continued*)

Element	Minimum Number of occurrences	Maximum Number of occurrences	Percentage
Aššur	50	76	17.0
Bêl	18	25	5.6
Bêlat-akkadi	1	1	0.2
Ber	5	6	1.3
Bur	2	2	0.4
Ea	1	1	0.2
Êkur } *Iâkku* }	2	4	0.9
Enlil	8	8	1.8
Idigla	3	9	2.0
Ilu	60	74	16.6
Ilâni	1	1	0 2
Ištar	2	4	0.9
Kubi	25	45	10 1
Marduk	12	14	3.2
Nabû	2	3	0.7
Ninurta	1	1	0.2
Papsukkal	2	2	0 4
Sîn	26	28	6.3
Šamaš	45	58	13.0
Šerua	11	16	3 6
Tašmetum	6	11	2.5
Tešup	1	1	0.2
Others	3	3	0 7

II The thirteenth century

Element	Minimum Number of occurrences	Maximum Number of occurrences	Percentage
Adad	65	86	18 0
Amurru	4	4	0 8
Mârat-Anim	1	1	0.2
Aššur	68	94	19.7
Bâbu	2	3	0 6
Bêl	16	19	4.0

II. The thirteenth century (*Continued*)

Element	Minimum Number of occurrences	Maximum Number of occurrences	Percentage
Bêlat-êkallim	1	1	0.2
Ber	10	11	2.3
Ea	3	3	0.6
Êkur } *Iâkku*	4	5	1.0
Enlil	8	8	1.7
Gula	2	2	0 4
Idigla	2	5	1.0
Ilu	38	48	10.0
Ilâni	6	9	1.9
Ištar	15	18	3.8
Kubi	8	11	2.3
Marduk	15	19	4.0
Nabû	7	7	1.5
Nergal	3	3	0.6
Ninua	1	1	0 2
Ninurta	4	4	0.8
Nusku	5	5	1.0
Papsukkal	2	2	0.4
Sîn	25	35	7.3
Šamaš	40	49	10.2
Šerua	2	8	1.7
Šulmânu	2	6	1.3
Tašmetum	5	6	1.3
Others	5	5	1 0

III. The twelfth century

Elemet	Minimum Number of occurrences	Meximum Number of occurrences	Percentage
Adad	20	23	23 5
Amurru	1	1	1.0
Anum	1	1	1.0
Aššur	17	18	18.3
Bâbu	1	1	1.0

III. The twelfth century (*Continued*)

Element	Minimum Number of occurrences	Maximum Number of occurrences	Percentage
Bêlat-êkallim	2	2	2.0
Ber	1	1	1.0
Enlil	1	1	1.0
Eru	2	2	2.0
Gula	3	3	3.1
Ilu	1	1	1.0
Ilâni	1	1	1.0
Ištar	5	5	5.1
Kubi	2	3	3.1
Marduk	7	9	9.2
Nabû	1	1	1.0
Ninurta	2	2	2.0
Nusku	1	1	1.0
Sakkil	1	1	1.0
Samnuḫa	1	3	3.1
Sîn	10	12	12.2
Šamaš	4	4	4.1
Šerua	1	2	2.0

I

The cosmopolitan tendency appears, firstly, in the growing use of the element "Adad" in Middle-Assyrian theophorous names. The worship of Adad, both in Assyria and Babylonia is attested from the oldest until the most recent times of Akkadian culture.[3] In the historical inscriptions of Assyria, he appears side by side with Aššur as the supreme god.[4] But in Old Assyrian times, the

[3] Cf the article "Adad," *RLA* I, pages 22 f ; Schlobies, H., *Der akkadische Wettergott in Mesopotamien* (*MAOG* I, Part 3), 1925.

[4] Cf. the formula "May Aššur and Adad hear his prayers, etc" For the time of Puzur-Aššur II, see Andrae, *Fest*, page 156, lines 13 f For the time of Aššur-rîm-nišêšu, see *KAH* I, 63, 14. In some cases, for a particular reason, an additional deity is added to the two supreme deities, thus, Bêl-šarri, on the occasion of the building of Aššur-uballiṭ's palace (*KAH* II, 27, 27) or Ištar-dînittum on the occasion of the dedication of her temple (*KAH* II, 28, 11 f) in the same reign.

predominance of Aššur was overwhelming. As a specifically Assyrian god, he appears in theophorous names more than three times as frequently as Ištar, five times as frequently as Sîn, and almost eight times as frequently as Adad.[5] In the fourteenth century, the use of "Aššur" still predominated, and the name of Šamaš preceded that of Adad A century later, however, "Adad" was employed almost as frequently as "Aššur" in theophorous names; and by the time of Ninurta-tukulti-Aššur, the name of Adad accounted for almost a quarter of all the theophorous names, and that of Aššur for less than twenty per cent.

That this development is to be explained on the basis of a growing cosmopolitanism seems fairly clear. Adad, as the old supreme deity, with no particularly local affiliations, would be more appealing than Aššur to the heterogeneous elements of a growing empire. Unlike Aššur, he does not appear as a god of conquest in the Middle-Assyrian onomasticon; only Aššur appears in such warlike names as "Aššur-mukanniš" (*KAJ* 162, 26) or "Aššur-mukaššid"[6] (*KAV* 209, 3); and such names are, in themselves, particularly infrequent. Perhaps, in this change, there is reflected a realization that the task of a conqueror extends beyond mere conquest to the systematic administration of the conquered territories.

The growing use of Ḫurrian elements within the Assyrian onomasticon points to the same cosmopolitan influences, and offers some confirmation of our conclusion The vast majority of the names in the Middle-Assyrian documents coming from Aššur are of Akkadian origin; and of these, the greater number are theophorous in formation. Nevertheless, a considerable number of names remain which are not to be explained on the basis of Akkadian; and in many cases Ḫurrian etymologies[7] have been

[5] Based on the Akkadian theophorous names of the Cappadocian tablets collected by F. J Stephens (*Personal Names*) Note also the corrections which are to be made to this list on the basis of Lewy, *OLZ* XXXIV, pages 343 ff

[6] In all probability, *ᵈEn-lil-KUR-id* of *KAJ* 7, 37, 42 is to be read "Enlil-kâšid" ("Enlil has arrived," referring to the image of Enlil on some festive occasion) The various occurrences of *Bal-ṭu-KUR-id* (Ebeling, *Eigennamen*, page 30) make this reading more likely than Ebeling's alternate suggestion of "Enlil-ukaššid" (*ibid*, page 38).

[7] For the relevant literature, see Ebeling, *Eigennamen*, pages 117 ff.

established or suggested. The significance of the occurrence of these names is, however, to be considered with caution.

In the first place, it is not always possible to decide whether or not the bearer of a foreign name is a native Assyrian or an immigrant living in Aššur. Evidently Melisaḫ, the son of Aššur-aḫ-iddina, grandson of Adad-šar-ilâni and great-grandson of Aššur-išmanni, is himself an Assyrian, despite his foreign name. On the other hand, the family of Zamutei̯a, whose son is called Ḫubite and whose grandsons are Išum-nâṣir and Apii̯au, are certainly not to be considered native Assyrians. Unfortunately, the choice is not always so easily made.

Despite these limitations, however, the following generalizations can be ventured. Ḫurrian influence becomes much more significant in Assyria in the thirteenth and twelfth centuries than it had been a hundred years earlier. To be sure in the reign of Aššur-uballiṭ, possibly two men of Ḫurrian[8] extraction had served as *lîmu*-officers.[9] But it is significant that the father in each case gave his son an Akkadian, though not specifically Assyrian, name. There are even two cases where children of Akkadian families may have received Ḫurrian names.[10] But together with one undoubtedly Ḫurrian family,[11] this is the extent of Ḫurrian influence, as it is revealed in our sources before the thirteenth century.

Before long, however, Ḫurrian influence becomes much more

[8] On the Ḫurrian etymologies of the names mentioned in this section, see Ebeling, *loc cit* , unless otherwise stated

[9] *Ibašši-ilu mâr Niruabi* (*KAJ* 12, 29 f , 63, 28) and *Rîmanni-Marduk mâr Tuttai̯a* (*KAJ* 24, 28 f , but cf note 48, below) Perhaps *Šumu-libši mâr Ardi-Tešup* (*KAJ* 41, 18, 154, 23) is a similar case of a Ḫurrian who receives an Akkadian name Lastly, Innamir, the son of Šururii̯a (*KAJ* 146, 19, 21, 35, 23, 26) may be an example of the same trend (On the reading in *KAJ* 35, see *HUCA* XXIV, p 213) Ebeling gives no suggested etymology for Šururia (*Eigennamen*, page 89) But the elements *Šur* (Clay, page 34), *Uri* (*ibid* , page 35) and i̯a (cf Gustavus, *AfO* XI, pages 146 ff) are known as components of Ḫurrian names The possibility of a Ḫurrian etymology for this name is thus to be considered.

[10] Katiri (*KAJ* 165, 1, 13, 21, 23) and Sarniqu (*KAJ* 170, 6, 11, 21, *KAV* 211, 28, 66)

[11] The family of Zamutei̯a mentioned above (*KAJ* 13, 1, 5 f)

marked. In the reigns of Adad-nirâri and his successors, not only slaves,[12] as would be expected, but persons in every walk of life bear Ḫurrian names. There are some, the names of whose relatives demonstrate that they are of Ḫurrian origin,[13] but others who are possibly Assyrians.[14] Two men bearing Ḫurrian names are themselves *lîmu*-officers,[15] and *Aḫlipi mâr Alguza*, who is undoubtedly of Ḫurrian extraction, serves as *hazi̇ânu* of Aššur (*KAJ* 103, 7 f ; 106, 6 f.). Needless to say, however, it remained fashionable for Ḫurrian fathers to find Assyrian names for their sons.[16]

Not only is the numerical advance significant, but there are qualitative differences also. In the fourteenth century, *Ibašši-ilu mâr Niruabi* and *Rîmanni Marduk mâr Tuttaja* presumably had had time to become "Akkadianized" before they served as *lîmu*-officers. Very likely they were born in an area where Akkadian culture predominated, and received their names at birth. In the later period, men who themselves bore Ḫurrian names served in high offices, and the interchange between Ḫurrian and Assyrian names within families becomes more marked. Perhaps the Assyrian merchant Melisaḫ, son of Aššur-aḫ-iddina, received his name as the result of a marriage of his father to a Kassite woman.[17] At any rate, his own father-in-law, a certain Batka, was doubtless a non-Assyrian, although the origin and significance of his name remain uncertain.[18]

[12] *KAJ* 245, 1–6, 8, 10 On the Ḫurrian origin of *Kilite* (line 6), cf Clay pages 31 (on the element *Kili*), 34 (on the ending *te*)

[13] The families of Šilme (*KAJ* 158, 22) Alguza (*KAJ* 10, 7 f ; 106, 6 f) No doubt, also, the participants of *KAJ* 124a, Irriuri of Ḫabḫa and Te(?)-ḫubšeni of Ḫusana, are native Ḫurrians.

[14] *Šenuni mâr Ber-šadûni* (*KAJ* 102, 10), *Girazu mâr Sîn-eriš* (*KAJ* 137, 16), and *Irrigi mâr Adadteja* (*KAJ* 168, 5)

[15] Sarniqu (*KAJ* 255, 14) and Agitešup (*KAJ* 137, 4) Note, also, the name of Ašti-uri, who is one of the subsidiaries of Bâbu-aḫ-iddina

[16] See *Burrari* (*KAJ* 159, rev 16), *Nirbija* (*KAJ* 75, 18), *Taḫinija* (*KAJ* 89, 21); *Talibbi* (*KAJ* 275, 5)

[17] This is the suggestion of Weidner (*AfO* XIII, page 122) See below, pages 127 ff for a discussion of the Kassite influence in this period

[18] On what basis Ebeling suggests precisely a "Subarian" etymology (*Eigennamen*, page 31) is not clear

The same trend becomes even more noticeable in the period of Ninurta-tukulti-Aššur. In the comparatively few documents coming from the twelfth century, a high incidence of Ḫurrian names is to be found. In part, of course, we are dealing with captive women (*W.* 100; cf. lines 5, 10, 31, 36, 37, 38), or other foreign women married to Assyrians.[19] But once again, we know of a *lîmu*-officer, Taḫulu (*KAJ* 126, end; 129, 19, perhaps belonging to this period), and of the father of a *lîmu*, Pauzi (*KAJ* 237, 15, etc.).[20] At least two of the important royal officials, Buza (*KAJ* 281, 7, etc.) and Mutta (*KAJ* 187, 10; etc.) have Ḫurrian names, as do other minor workmen who were employed by the court.[21] The *abarakku* of the household of a Bâbu-aḫ-iddina has a Ḫurrian name.[22] And such personages as Kuda (*W.* 107, 3; *Assur* 12758, 4) and Qabianu[23] (*KAJ* 264, 8; *W.* 102, 4) are among the many who offer *namurâte* to the king

The impetus which is shown in the worship of Adad, who is the Assyrian equivalent of the Ḫurrian god, Tešup,[24] is, therefore, a reflection of the same cosmopolitan trend, and is closely connected with the growing influence of Ḫurrian culture. The basic conceptions of the pantheon appear slowly to have been adapted to the new importance which Adad receives. Starting with the thirteenth century, he began to be regarded more and more, together with Aššur, as the distinctive god of the nation or empire. In the fourteenth century, only Aššur is mentioned in names which reflect a particular relationship with his people.[25]

[19] Thus, Kizaia (*KAJ* 192, 27, 209, 6, *W* 80, 9, 103, 4), and, no doubt, Salâ (*W* 63, 5)

[20] Perhaps the name is connected with the city-name, Pa'uzi, known, from the Annals of Adad-nirâri II, to have been situated in the territory of Hanigalbat (*KAH* II, 84, 39 f) Since the conquest of this territory was undertaken in the reign of Shalmaneser I (*KAH* I, 13, 18), such cultural influence may be readily comprehended

[21] Butaiaza (*KAJ* 185, 9), Urḫaia (*KAJ* 189, 11), Note, also, *ᶠḪasi-AN PA-ri-gi* (*KAJ* 192, 12)

[22] Bulali (*W* 90 7 f etc).

[23] On the element *Qa-ba*, cf Clay, page 33 For *–iânu*, cf *ibid*, page 31

[24] See Meyer, volume 1, Part II, 481, 490 on the identity of Hadad and Tešub Cf , also, Tallqvist, *Gotterep* , page 471, *s v.* Te-eš-su-ub

[25] *Aššur-bêl-nišêšu* (*KAJ* 8, 38, 162, 2, 8, 172, 3), *Aššur-mupaḫḫir-nišêšu* (*KAJ* 143, 13).

In the thirteenth century, however, a change is apparent. Despite the increased extent of the sources, Aššur appears in only one such name.[26] Adad, on the other hand, is known in the names of this period as the "shepherd," "mountain," and "ruler" of the people,[27] in the last case, there may be as many as three distinct individuals whose names honor the god Adad in this way.[28]

II

The vicissitudes of the cults of Sîn and Šamaš in the Middle-Assyrian period point to a similar, if more complex, development. In the Old Assyrian period, the popularity of the moon god seems to have followed that of only Aššur and his consort, Ištar.[29] But for some reason, the cult of Sîn suffered a decline in the early Middle-Assyrian period. On the evidence of the proper names and likewise of historical inscriptions,[30] the popularity of Šamaš-worship is shown to have surpassed considerably that of Sîn. Perhaps Šamaš, the potential warrior, appealed more to the Assyrians of these early centuries, than his peaceful colleague, Sîn.[31]

---

[26] *Aššur-šad-nišêšu* (*CT* XXXIII, 14b, 8).

[27] *Adad-re'u-nišê* (*KAJ* 120, 30), *Adad-šad-nišêšu* (*KAJ* 145, 10), *Adad-šar-nišê* (*KAJ* 83, 7, 217, 10; 308, 3).

[28] It should be noted that in Neo-Assyrian times, the trend is completely reversed Cf the indexes to Waterman, *Royal Correspondence*, Part IV, pages 157 f

[29] Stephens, *op cit*

[30] On Arık-dên-ılu's renewal of the temple of Šamaš, his tutelary deity, see *KAH* II, 29 Šamaš, but not Sîn, is always listed among the deities aiding Adad-nirârı (*KAH* I, 3, 12, II, 35, 9, etc) and Tukultı-Nınurta (*KAH* II, 58, 49) in their victories (In *KAH* II, 60, 15, where Tukultı-Nınurta is called the beloved of Sîn, it is only as part of a catalogue of such designations, in which numerous other deities are mentioned)

[31] On the fierce nature of Šamaš, see, in addition to these historical inscriptions, Ebeling *AfO* XIV, pages 299 ff , where he publishes a Middle-Assyrian fragment of the Etana myth, in which Šamaš is invoked to fulfill a potential curse Note also, that Aššur-nâdın-aplı raises his hands to Šamaš and Aššur when the Tıgrıs overflows a large area of Aššur, regarding these as the deities to be propitiated (Stephens, *YBT* IX, 71, lines 15 ff ; cf Weidner,

However, with the developing cosmopolitanism of the later Middle-Assyrian period, the trend is halted and reversed. Perhaps the fall of Ḫarrân to the Assyrians may have played a minor role in the development. The earliest mention of the conquest of Ḫarrân comes from the reign of Adad-nirâri,[32] but the more definitive annexation probably took place in the reign of his successor, Shalmaneser I.[33] To be sure the city did not remain in Assyrian hands after the death of Tukulti-Ninurta.[34] But the memory of the conquest must have remained with the Assyrians, to reveal itself in the onomasticon of the succeeding generations. As is to be expected, the effects of such developments are not seen immediately, if only because a generation must elapse before a child who is named in honor of a historical event becomes known in business or administrative documents. Moreover, in the Middle-Assyrian period, we have little evidence concerning the years immediately following the reign of Tukulti-Ninurta, and must wait until the period of Ninurta-tukulti-Aššur before we have full documentation of any such tendencies. But by his reign, the development is clearly discernible. The percentage of theophorous names bearing the element *Sîn* is, in this

"Eine Bauinschrift des Konigs Assurnadinapli," *AfO* VI, page 13) Cf, also, Tallqvist, *Gotterep*, pages 453 ff

On the mild character of the god Sîn, see Tallqvist, *op. cit.*, pages 442 ff.

[32] *KAH* I, 5, 13

[33] *KAH* I, 13, col. III, 4 Mentioning a specific campaign rather than listing the city among a group of conquered territories, the inscription of Shalmaneser gives the impression of at least a more systematic attempt to bring Ḫarran under Assyrian suzerainty To be sure, as early as the reign of Tukulti-Ninurta, Assyria had claimed the conquest of Sippar (*KAH* II, 61, 14), and a corresponding influence of Šamaš upon the Assyrian onomasticon might have been expected. But one may doubt how successfully Tukulti-Ninurta was able to impose Assyrian rule upon the city of the sun god, and in any case, the brevity of the Assyrian domination, which must have ended before the death of Tukulti-Ninurta (see below, note 34), as well as the geographical situation of the city, would tend to make its religious influence more remote than the influence of Ḫarran It is reasonable, therefore, to explain the increase in the Sîn-cult on the basis of the conquest of Ḫarran as well as upon the new cosmopolitan religious orientation

[34] Weidner, *Studien zur Chron*, page 75, Winckler, pages 334 ff Cf, also, Weidner, *AfO* X, pages 19 ff, on the extent of Assyrian power at the time of Ninurta-tukulti-Aššur.

period, almost twice the figure for the fourteenth century,[35] and the influence of Šamaš is correspondingly low.

The increasing importance of Marduk in the same period should likewise be attributed to this growing cosmopolitanism. In Cappadocian times, the worship of Marduk by Assyrians is unknown.[36] His influence appears first in Middle-Assyrian times, and grows somewhat more marked in the reign of Ninurta-tukulti-Aššur.

Despite the assertion of Weidner, however, no immediate evidence of such an impetus appears in the reign of Tukulti-Ninurta. Babylonian influence in Assyria was already appreciable before his reign; and the evidence suggests that the conquest of Babylon was, perhaps, less decisive, in its cultural implications, than the conquest of Ḫarrân.

The close relationship between Assyria and Babylon in the days of Aššur-uballiṭ is known from the Synchronous History.[37] Karaḫardaš, ruler of Babylon, was the offspring of a diplomatic alliance between the daughter of Aššur-uballiṭ and a Babylonian king. It is not surprising, therefore, that in the reign of Aššur-uballit, two *lîmu*-officers should have been named with "Marduk" as divine element,[38] or that another *lîmu* should have been the son of a Šuzub-Marduk [39] Even the divine element *Bêlat-Akkadı* occurs not in the reign of Tukulti-Ninurta, as Weidner had suspected,[40] but once again in the reign of Aššur-uballiṭ.[41] Quite

[35] Note also the frequent offerings made to Sîn in this period (for the references, see Ebeling, *Eigennamen*, page 103)

[36] Stephens, *op cit*, cf page 98 The name Marduk is also entirely lacking in the few documents which have been dated in the fifteenth century.

[37] *Synchr Hist* I, 8–17

[38] *KAJ* 24, 28 (Rîmanni-Marduk) and *KAJ* 175, 46 (Marduk-nâdin-aḫi)

[39] Adad-mušêzib; see *KAJ* 13, 35, etc It may also be noted that an additional Mušêzib-Marduk, not accounted in the tables at the beginning of this chapter, occurs in an undated tablet, *KAJ* 251 However, the eponymy of this tablet, Aššur-eriš (line 12), makes it likely that the document comes either from the reign of Aššur-uballit (cf *KAJ* 157, 15; *HUCA* XXIV, p 208) or from that of Adad-nirâri (cf *KAV* 96, 19, *ibid*, p 228) Thus we have one more such name which appears to come from a time preceding the reign of Tukulti-Ninurta

[40] *AfO* XIII, page 121

[41] Thus the name *Silli*[li]*-be-el-ta-ka-di*, *KAJ* 165, 25. On the dating of this tablet, see *HUCA* XXIV, pp 206 f

in consonance with this situation is the fact that in the same reign, a royal scribe,[42] clearly of Babylonian origin,[43] should find it necessary, at some period of his residence in Aššur, to dedicate a shrine to his patron, Marduk. In fact, the cultural influence of Babylon upon Assyria in the reign of Aššur-uballiṭ is evident both from our juridical sources and from the historical documents already known.

The meager influence of the Kassites throughout the Middle-Assyrian period gives us additional reason to believe that the conquest of Babylon by Tukulti-Ninurta did not have the decisive cultural influence which Weidner suggested. Ebeling notes only four, or possibly five, Kassite names in the Middle-Assyrian documents Of these, Melišugab (*KAJ* 134, 13, 22) belongs in the fourteenth century,[44] while Melisaḫ and Meliḫarbe (*KAJ* 62, 22) come from the succeeding century in the reign of Shalmaneser. Only Induri̯a (*W.* 100, 32), among all those for whose names Ebeling suggests the possibility of a Kassite etymology, comes from a period following Tukulti-Ninurta's conquest of Babylon. Beyond these names, it should be noted that the name *Kaššu* or *Kaššiu* is known from the thirteenth century (*KAJ* 98, 16, 21, 244, 16) and from the time of Ninurta-tukulti-Aššur (*W.* 72, 4, 13). But this is the extent of Kassite influence, as it can so far be traced, on the Middle-Assyrian onomasticon.

Our tablets therefore give little evidence of any cultural influence exerted by the Kassite captives, even though their presence in Aššur in definitely established after the campaigns of Tukulti-Ninurta.[45] Nor has Weidner proved his hypothesis that the captive Kassite king served as an Assyrian *lîmu* in the same reign It is by no means certain that *VAT* 8722,[46] which has as *lîmu Kaš-ti-li-a-šu* (line 30) must come from the reign of Tukulti-

[42] See the document published in *AKA*, pages 388 f

[43] On the basis of his name, (line 1) *Marduk-nâdin-aḫḫê* (line 2) *mâr Marduk-uballiṭ mâr Uššur-ana-Marduk*

[44] Note also that the Kara[ḫardaš] of *KAV* 97, 1, is probably the grandson of Aššur-uballit, known from the Synchronistic History (cf note 47, below)

[45] See Weidner, *AfO* XIII, pages 122 f

[46] *Ibid*, Plate VII

Ninurta. It has already been shown that the designation of Kâr-Tukulti-Ninurta (*ibid.*, line 6) may have been in use as late as the reign of Ninurta-tukulti-Aššur (see above, p 115 note 26). The Kassite name of the *limu* of this tablet may therefore be nothing more than one of the few examples of minor Kassite influence, which can be traced from the fourteenth century, and which was scarcely affected by the campaigns of Tukulti-Ninurta.

If we attribute the Babylonian cultural influence upon Assyria to the factors which had been operating since the time of Aššur-uballiṭ, the meagerness of Kassite influence is not difficult to explain. It is known that in the reign of Aššur-uballiṭ, the Assyrians found themselves particularly hostile to the Kassite elements of Babylon.[47] Moreover, the northward migration of Babylonians during the period of Kassite domination, and the settlement of large numbers of them in Assyrian territory,[48] offer a clear explanation of the cultural development within Assyria. On the other hand, if the campaigns of Tukulti-Ninurta were principally responsible for any religious rapprochement between the two peoples, we should at least expect that the Kassite influence might be, in some degree, comparable to that of the Babylonians, even allowing for the fact that their culture might initially be stranger, and less esteemed by a Semitic

[47] *Synchr Hist*, *loc cit* Cf *AKA*, pages xxiv, f Even though Karaḫardaš and Kurigalzu received Kassite names, they were looked upon as grandsons of Aššur-uballit, and the opposition to them came from the Kassites, who resented any possibility of Assyrian domination of Babylon Since such hostility existed, it is not surprising that, despite Babylonian influence in Assyria, any corresponding Kassite influence is hardly discernible

[48] Cf *AKA*, Introduction, pages xxi ff Part of the earlier Ḫurrian influence in the Middle-Assyrian period may also be connected with this northward migration of Babylonians (On the considerable Ḫurrian influence in Babylonia during the Kassite period, cf Clay, pages 28 ff As an indication of such a connection, note the name of the *limu* of *KAJ* 24, 28 f, *Rîmanni-Marduk mâr Tuttaja* A different etymology of the name Tuttaja, however, may be suggested by the bye-name of Marduk, *Tu-tu*; see Tallqvist, *Gotterep*, page 472)

Nevertheless, the vastly increased Ḫurrian influence of the later centuries is, as has been suggested, part of a broader development within the Assyrian empire

people.[49] Since, as a matter of fact, the cultural contacts between Assyria and Babylon can be shown to have existed before the time of Tukulti-Ninurta, it is clear that the migration of the Babylonians into Assyria in the Kassite period gives us the best explanation of these phenomena. The conquest of Babylon, like the conquest of Ḫarrân, undoubtedly played its part. But it should be remembered that Babylon remained under Assyrian domination for a much shorter period of time than Ḫarrân, and for this reason, also, Tukulti-Ninurta's victory can scarcely have had the cultural importance which Weidner tended to attribute to it.

A further suggestion of Weidner's[50] must be briefly mentioned. In the general period of Tukulti-Ninurta's reign, the divine element, Marduk, is found to recur within the same family, and such repetition is also taken by Weidner as a further sign of the pervasive influence of Marduk-worship. However, we need not suppose any greater enthusiasm for Marduk when a child is named Kidin-Marduk in consonance with the name of his grandfather, Uballiṭsu-Marduk (*KAJ* 110, 22 f.)[51] than when the same name is given without such motivation (e. g., *KAJ* 165, 7). As a matter of fact, it might mean precisely the contrary of what Weidner is trying to show: if we had similar information for the earlier period, even the slightly increased frequency of the use of the element *Marduk* in the thirteenth century might prove illusory; or, alternately, the families in which the element *Marduk* recurs might be natives of Babylon living in Assyria, and precisely these should be excluded in any attempt to examine the Babylonian cultural influence upon the native Assyrians.

It appears, therefore, that the suggestion of Weidner cannot be maintained on the basis of a strict chronological analysis of

[49] For the extent to which Kassite influence is reflected in the Babylonian onomasticon of this time, see Clay, pages 36 ff

[50] *Loc cit*, pages 121 ff

[51] Regarding the other instances of such recurrences of the name Marduk quoted by Weidner (*KAJ* 72, 6–8, 93, 20 f), the one is found in a document which is to be assigned to the reign of Shalmaneser and not of Tukulti-Ninurta, and the other in a document which may, with equal likelihood, be dated in either of the two reigns

the Middle-Assyrian contracts The growing influence of Marduk-worship in thirteenth-century Assyria is not solely the result of Tukulti-Ninurta's conquest of Babylon, but of a gradual process of religious development And as ın the case of the worship of Sîn, the full results of all the processes become apparent in the tıme of Nınurta-tukulti-Aššur. Broadly speaking, Marduk may be considered, beginning with the fourteenth century, as a mınor, but still significant element of the Assyrıan pantheon. The constant impetus which hıs worship receives is one aspect of a growing cosmopolitanism, and of the absorption within the Assyrian pantheon, of the gods of the immediate environment.

III

The very apparent decline in the use of *DINGIR* as a theophorous element between the fourteenth and twelfth centuries seems to reflect the same religious tendencies. The process is not unique in Assyria. Stamm notes the same development in Babylonıan names starting with the Kassite period [52] But perhaps the best explanation of the phenomenon can be found in the relıgious development which we have already noted in Assyria

Certainly the widespread use of *DINGIR* in fourteenth-century names does not reflect one specific cult or religious belief. A great number of the names in which it occurs call upon god in complaint or petitıon.[53] It is psychologically understandable, and perhaps less presumptuous towards the partıcular deity involved, that in such cases one should substitute for hıs name the general expression, "O god," or "my god." Beyond this, many, and perhaps most, of these names are undoubtedly to be read in the form *ılı* ("my god") rather than *ılu* ("O god") [54] A number of indıcations point to this conclusion. If *DINGIR* were always to be read *ılu*, then such names as *DINGIR-nûr-*

[52] *Op. cıt*, page 72

[53] E g, *Dugul-ılı, Ilı-nashıra, Admatı-ılı, Atanah-ılı, Ma'ı-ılı, Uqa-dên-ılı* Cf Stamm, *op cıt*, page 74

[54] On the suggested readıngs for other perıods, cf Stamm, pages 70 ff, and the lıterature there referred to

ilâni (*KAJ* 47, 34)[55] would be incomprehensible The following orthographic evidence should also be noted:

1) Other personal suffixes are added to *ilu* during this period (cf. *Ṣilli-iluka*, *Šumma-ilunu*, *Ilušu-bani*, *Ilušu-nammir*, and others).

2) In the genitive, where the personal suffix of the first person can be clearly seen, the form *iliịa* is attested (*Aba-iliịa*, *Nûr-iliịa*, *Zika-šar-iliịa*. Note also the *lîmu* of the time of Adad-nirâri I, Itti-iliịa-šamšu, Andrae, *Fest.*, page 159).

3) In the genitive without personal suffix, where the form *ili* is required, it is always written *DINGIR* (*Ammar-ša-ili*, *Innamar-dên-ili*, *Itti-ili-balâtu*).

We should expect on the basis of 1) and 2) that the expression *ili* ("my god," *nominative*) would likewise occur in these texts; and on the basis of 3), that it may be written simply as *DINGIR*.[56] On the other hand, the examples given under 3) make it clear that the term *ilu* without personal ending occurs in these texts in the sense of "a god" (cf. *Ibašši-ilu*) or "the god "

Perhaps the element *EN*, the use of which underwent a comparable decline in the later Middle-Assyrian period, may likewise stand for a common noun with the suffix of the first person singular. The evidence here is not so compelling as in the case of *DINGIR*. Nevertheless, a few indications may be found. The spelling *be-li* ("my lord") is known to occur elsewhere in Akkadian sources[57] Moreover, in the Middle-Assyrian period, where the noun "*bêl*" is clearly in the genitive case, it is marked with the suffix of the first person singular.[58] Thus, since the spelling "*be-li*" never occurs in these texts, it may be ventured

[55] Concerning Ebeling's listing of a similar name, *Ilu-kidin-ilâni*, see the Appendix

[56] On the reading of *AN*=*ili*=*il₆* for the Old Assyrian period, see Lewy, *KTS*, page 68; *OLZ*, 1929, column 173

[57] Stamm, *op cit* For references, see the Index of personal names Note also the feminine forms in such names as *ᶠBe-el-ti-ba-ni-ti* (*ibid* , page 312), etc

[58] The only case in these sources appears to be Ṭâb-šar-bêli-ịa (*KAV* 111, 4)

that *EN* itself may stand for the expression *bêli* ("my lord"). Once again, therefore, we may be dealing with a theophorous element which is used as a substitution not for one specific deity but for various gods, depending on the family and circumstances in which the name is used.

The problem why this process of substitution should have become so much less prevalent with the advance of the centuries is to be approached on the basis of these considerations. If the expressions "my god" or "my lord" had reference to specific family cults rather than to those of the major deities, we should clearly be witnessing a trend which parallels the other developments towards a religious cosmopolitanism. With the expanding cultural empire of Assyria, and the growing popularity of neighboring religious cults, a corresponding decline in the more particularistic cults of private groups and families is only to be expected.

A further example of the decline in the worship of private family deities in the late Middle-Assyrian period may be discerned in the history of the cult of Kubi. The precise nature of this cult has not been established. But Thureau-Dangin has shown that the common noun ***kûbu*** is to be translated "foetus",[59] and on the basis of this translation, Stamm takes the theophorous element to have reference to a previous premature stillbirth [60]

Names mentioning the divine element Kubi are not limited to Assyria. Several such names are known among the Babylonians of Nuzi[61] and of the Kassite period.[62] In the Old-Assyrian period, also, they are by no means uncommon.[63] However, the tremendous importance which the cult must have occupied in the fifteenth and fourteenth centuries, when it accounted for some ten per cent of all theophorous names, contrasts sharply with its

[59] "Notes Assyriologiques," *RA* XIX, pages 81 f

[60] *Op cit*, page 306.

[61] Gelb, Purves and MacRae, page 23 (*Apil-Kube*), page 91 (*Kubi-eriš*, *Kubi-šarri*), page 108 (*Nûr-Kubi*); and several others

[62] Clay, *op cit*, page 84 (*Iddin-Kubi*), page 100 (*Kubi-ilu*), page 57 (*Ardi-^{d}AZAG-BI*), etc

[63] Stephens, p 43 (*I-din-Ku-be*, etc, to be read *I-dí-Ku-be*, etc, cf Lewy, *OLZ* XXXIV, 344 f), p 50 (Irad-Kube), p 52 (Kubiia), p 66 (Šu-Kubim), p 68 (Urad-Kubim), etc

reduced significance in the succeeding centuries. Once again, the most probable explanation is to be sought in the expansion of empire, and the choice of foreign gods to replace the old family deities, in whose honor a large part of the religious efforts of the Assyrians must hitherto have been directed.

Equally difficult to interpret is the precise significance of the various fluctuations undergone, apparently, by the cult of Ištar in the Old and Middle-Assyrian periods. At first sight, the cult of Ištar appears to have received a considerable set-back during the centuries between the Cappadocian and Middle-Assyrian periods. In the Cappadocian tablets, the influence of Ištar is second only to that of Aššur, her consort,[64] whereas throughout the Middle-Assyrian period, Ištar appears to be only a minor deity.

On the other hand, part of the difference is to be explained by the fact that Ištar, as a female god, was, in particular, the deity to be praised or invoked in the naming of a daughter. In early Middle-Assyrian documents, especially, we encounter comparatively few women. It would be rash, therefore, to draw far-reaching conclusions concerning the cult of Ištar on the basis of our evidence. On the other hand, a gradual increase in Ištar-worship may be indicated within the Middle-Assyrian period itself[65] Perhaps here also, we are witnessing the effects of early Assyrian imperialism on the pantheon. It is possible, at any rate, in view of the limited extent of the Ištar cult in the fourteenth century, that the later texts are dealing not with the spouse of Aššur,[66] but with some of the various Ištar's who are worshipped

[64] *Ibid*

[65] The more frequent appearance of women in the later documents will not explain the growing use of the element *Ištar* even in men's names in the thirteenth and twelfth centuries

[66] The oldest forms of Ištar-worship in Aššur insolved Ištar of Aššur and Ištar of Nineveh, together with some subsidiary goddesses, named Ištar, whose shrines were in the same temples as those of the great goddesses The temple of Ištar of Aššur was built in the reign of Ilušuma, and restored several times before the often-mentioned restoration of Tukulti-Ninurta I (*KAH* II, 20, 5 ff , 34, 6 ff , 42, 5 ff , 48, 9 ff). Apparently, Ištar-dînittum was worshipped in a shrine within *Eanna*, the temple of the Assyrian Ištar

throughout the area of Assyrian influence. Thus, when specific sacrifices to Ištar are mentioned in the reign of Ninurta-tukulti-Aššur, they are explicitly offered to Ištar of Arba'-ili[67] or else to the *Ištar ša šamê*.[68]

* * * *

These, then, are the developments which affected the Assyrian pantheon in the centuries which constitute the Middle-Assyrian period. Sometimes clearly, and sometimes only as a possible interpretation, they reveal a development towards assimilation and cosmopolitanism which we might expect in an incipient empire. Ancient religion is both tolerant and conservative. The recognition of a new deity does not imply the rejection of the old. Gods die slowly in the Ancient World, even after senility has shown its symptoms. In the course of three hundred years, there were no violent changes, only gradual trends.

It is only by close attention to gradual trends, however, that any form of human development is to be understood. That these few detailed observations may shed some light upon the history of Assyrian religion is the hope in which they are presented.

(cf. *KAH* II, 48, 25 and 49, 21; note also that the shrine of Ištar-dînittum was likewise founded by Ilušuma; see *KAH* II, 52, 5 ff)

The temple of Ištar of Nineveh was founded somewhat later by Maništušu, the son of Šarru-kên (*Liverpool Annals*, XIX, page 105; for full references, see H and J. Lewy, *HUCA* XVII, page 72, note 308), and was frequently restored, by Šamši-Adad I and later kings. A temple or shrine of Ištar-annunaitum is also mentioned, in an inscription of Tukulti-Ninurta, as stemming from early times (*KAH* II, 50, 5 ff)

[67] *W.* 76, 6

[68] *W.* 89, 8

APPENDIX

CORRECTIONS TO EBELING'S *EIGENNAMEN*

Ebeling's collection of Middle-Assyrian proper names has been an invaluable aid in the preparation of this study. Nevertheless, a more detailed analysis of the documents has required a modification of many of his conclusions and suggestions. A number of the following corrections to his work have been discussed above. For the sake of convenience in the use of his helpful volume, however, they are summarized here. The more necessary corrections of misprints, etc. are also made. Where Ebeling has merely quoted the wrong line of a text, or failed to mention the re-appearance of a person already listed in the same tablet, no notation has been made. For the sake of convenience, however, an indication is given in those cases where names are omitted from their position in alphabetic order, even though these names were correctly read by Ebeling, and given elsewhere in his book.

No explanation of the corrections is given where merely a matter of textual transliteration is concerned, or where the problem has been discussed elsewhere in this study. In other cases, corrections are justified in the footnotes.

For the purposes of this classification, differences in spelling of the same name have been ignored.

It should also be noted that, particularly in the case of frequently occurring names, Ebeling has listed, in the final rubric under the name in question, all isolated references which cannot be identified on the basis of a patronymic or through some other means. It will be seen that it has been necessary, on occasion, to suggest changes also in these rubrics of miscellaneous readings.

Page 4

S. v. Abattu (1)	*After* 316, 21, *add* (?).
Add Abattu (3)	S. d. Adad-šumu-lîšir 89, 23; 316, 21 (?).
S. v. Abazia	*Read* A-zu-zi-ḭa.[1]

[1] Ebeling reads *Abazia* in 18, 6 (*Eigennamen*, page 4) but he refers to this reading as *Amazia* in identifying the same man in 149, 9, where, however, he reads his name as *Azuni* (*ibid.*, page 30)

Page 5

S. v Abi-ilu (2)	*Delete* E. D. [i-g]a-ia-a[-e?][2]
S. v. Abi-ilu (4) *and* (17)	*The references in both of these rubrics are to the same person.*
S. v. Abi-ilu (12)	*Add ? after* auch 27, 1, 5.[3]
S. v. Abi-ilu (19)	*Delete S.* 210, 6 f.[4]
S. v. Abuḫia[5] (3) *and* (4)	*The references in both of these rubrics are to the same person.*[6]

Page 6

S. v. Abu-ṭâbu[7] (6)	*Add* 139, 5, 18; *which is to be deleted from rubric 14 (see* HUCA *XXIV, p 191).*
S. v. Abu-ṭâbu (14)	*Separate S.* 119, 1, *and add* S. d. Ṣâbê-^{d}Ištar.[8]

However, the reading *A-zu-z[i-ia]* for 149, 9 seems very plausible, and since the man referred to as Abazija in 18, 6 is undoubtedly the same person, we cannot be sure which of the texts gives the better reading Despite this uncertainty, since the name *Azuzija* is known elsewhere in these texts, we have assumed that this is the correct reading in *KAJ* 18, also, and that a wedge was omitted from the sign for *zu* in this name

[2] Ebeling's presumably reads 64, 24, as:

mâr A-šur-qarrad [mâr I-g]a-ia-a[-e?]

(cf 26, 7) The correct reading, however, must be:

mâr A-šur-qarrâd [uraḫ q]ar-ra'-a-[tu]

There is no evidence to connect this Aššur-qarrâd with the son of Igajâu

[3] The genealogy of 27, 5 seems to be

Ṭâb-[.]-^{d} Šamaš?
↓
[.]-a-ḫi
↓
Abi-ilu

The traces of the grandfather's name are not those of Urad-Kube

[4] Although *KAJ* 173=*KAV* 210 (*VAT* 8995), Ebeling gives the Abi-ilu who appears in the former as the son of Adad-nirâri (page 4, *s v* Abi-ilu), while he lists him in the latter without patronymic in a miscellaneous entry, (rubric 19)

[5] Lewy tentatively suggests the reading Apuhija (=In exchange with me)

[6] *KAJ* 50 is one of the many instances where a relative of the debtor, here the brother, acts as witness to a transaction

[7] Read, better, *Abu-ṭâb*

[8] Cf. *Eigennamen*, page 78, where, however, Ṣâbê-Ištar is given as the father of Aḫu(sic!)-ṭâbu

S v. Adad-aḫ-iddina (2)	*Read* Adad-[ ], *and delete* 81, 6 [9]
Page 7	
S. v. Adad-bêl-gabbe (1)	*Omit* ša eli mât rap-ḫa-ia-e *and* 212, 2. *Add this title and reference as a separate listing under* (3).
S. v. Adad-bêl-ilâni	*Separate the two references* S. *19 cannot be dated, and there is no basis for identification.*
S. v. Adad-bêl-uṣur (1) *and* (2)	*The references in both of these rubrics are to the same person.*[10]
Add ᵈAdad-bi-ir-ti	57, 5.
S v. Adad-da(mm)eq (1)	*There is no reason for Ebeling's identification of 34, 19 and 34, 24. List the latter separately under* (8).
Page 9	
S. v. Adad-mušêzib (1)	*Delete* auch [58, 35]?, *which belongs under* (3).

[9] Of course, the Adad-[ ] of 56, 6, being the son of Iqîšeja, cannot also be the son of Dajjânija (81, 6) The identification of these two men must be a careless afterthought of Ebeling The reconstruction of the name of Adad-aḫ-iddina in *KAJ* 56, therefore, has no basis Nor is there more cogency in Ebeling's alternate reading of Adad-šamši (page 10) Even if the name Dajjânija (cf *KAJ* 56, 1) could be identified with Dajjânu (*KAJ* 11, 23, etc), chronological considerations would completely rule out the identification of *Dajjânija mâr Adad-*[ ] (time of Adad-nirâri or Shalmaneser) with the *Dajjânu mâr Adad-šamši* who lived in the time of Aššur-uballit

[10] Despite the different spelling, the same man is intended He is an official who, from time to time, receives a single sheep from the king for the purpose of a sacrifice Thus in *KAJ* 187, of the twenty sheep given as a *namurtu* to the king, nineteen are entrusted to Muttu (line 10) or to Šamaš-nûr (line 12) for tending, and the remaining animal is given to Adad-bêl-usur Again, in *KAJ* 201, we learn of a single sheep received in the house of Adad-bêl-usur for a sacrifice, and it is reported (incidentally) that two days later, another sheep was given to the lions *KAJ* 221 gives a similar account of a sheep given to the house of Adad-bêl-usur and to the lions, while in *W* 89, Adad-bêl-usur brings forth one sheep from his house at the royal command That these all refer to the same person, despite the variant spelling of *KAJ* 221, cannot be doubted Probably *W* 103 refers to him also, although, since the text is incomplete, full certainty cannot be attained Note also *KAJ* 205, where Adad-bêl-usur appears among a list of those to whom sheep are distributed from among the *namurâte* brought to the king

S. v. Adad-mušêzıb (3) and (7) — *The references in both of these rubrics are to the same person. Cf. Ebeling, page 89, s. v. Šuzub-Marduk (2).*

S. v Adad-mušêzib (4) and (6) — *The references in both of these rubrics are to the same person. Cf. note 6.*

Page 10

S. v. Adad-rîṣuia (1) — *Delete all references after 100, 32 (see the previous entry,* Adad-rîm-ilâni).

S. v Adad-šamšı (1) and (5) — *The references in both of these rubrics are probably to the same person* (HUCA XXIV, pp. 245 f.).

S. v. Adad-šamšı (4) — *Delete 56, 6 (see s. v.* Adad-aḫ iddina, *rubric 2).*

Page 11

S. v. Adad-šımani (1) and (2) — *The references in both of these rubrics are to the same person.*[11]

S. v. Adad-šum-iddina (2) — *Delete W. 88, 2, and add as a separate entry, s. v. (4).*[12]

S. v. Adad-šum-ıddina (3) — *Delete 118, 9 (*amêl âlik urkı)*, and add as a separate entry,* s. v. (5). *Retain 213, 7 (=2).*[13]

S v. Adad-šum-iddina — *Add* (6) Father of Upru, 263, 5.[14]

---

[11] Once again, despite the different spelling In *W* 88 and *W* 101 Adad-šımanı ıs mentioned as an *alaḫḫınu* In *KAJ* 283, his name ıs included among a list of men known as $^{am\hat{e}l}$a-laḫ-ḫı-nı ù $^{am\hat{e}l}$bappırî (lines 10 f).

[12] In *W* 88, 2, Adad-šum-ıddına offers a *namurtu* of five sheep, which ıs disposed of to various officials He is said to have come from Suḫi. In the remaining tablets, he is one of the $^{am\hat{e}l}$bappırû, who receive grants, generally of a single sheep, from the kıng

[13] Note the dating of these tablets There ıs no reason for ıdentıfyıng an $^{am\hat{e}l}$alık urkı in the service of Melisaḫ with one of the royal $^{am\hat{e}l}$bappırû of Ninurta-tukultı-Aššur.

[14] Apparently more ın harmony with the traces than Ebeling's readıng: [A-šu]r-šum-ıddına

S. v. Adad-šumu-rabbi (2)	*Omit* "S. d. mâr (d)adad"[15] *and* "= 1".[16]
S. v. Adad-šumu-lîši (1)	*Read* V. d. Abattu u. Adad-šamši, 56, 30; 89, 23.
S. v. Adad-šumu-rabbi (2) *and* (3)	*The references in both of these rubrics are to the same person.*[17]
Page 12	
S v. Adadteia (2)	*Add* 275, 3 (!).[18]
S. v. Adad-tûra	*Read* (1) 214, 10, 237, 2; *W* 78, 8 (?). (2) *S.* 99, 7; *S.* 109, 7, *S.* 200a, 8.[19]
S. v. Adad-zêr-iddina (1) *and* (2)	*The references in both of these rubrics are to the same person.*
Page 13	
S. v. Admati-ilu (3)	*Remove* 16, 26, *and add to* (2).[20] *The remaining names of this rubric are, of course, a miscellaneous grouping.*
S. v. Admati-ilu	*Add* (4) 242, 4 (?). *A possible reading.*
Page 14	
S. v. Aḫu-ṭâbu (2)[21]	*Delete* 21, 31.[22]

15 What is Ebeling's source for this patronymic?

16 Once again, since the date of *KAV* 19 is not to be determined, there is no means of identifying the Adad-šuma-rabbi of this tablet

17 The two men are to be identified, despite the different spelling of their names *KAJ* 189 describes the ***namurtu*** of Adad-šuma-rabbi to the king *KAJ* 212 speaks of the ***namurtu*** of ^{nâr}*Zu-ḫi-na-ia* after the death of Adad-šuma-rabbi Since *KAJ* 212 was written several months later than *KAJ* 189 it seems likely that the same Adad-šuma-rabbi is referred to

18 The following reconstruction of *KAJ* 275, 2 f , seems plausible

(line 2) ^{m}*Ki-[din-Sîn]* (line 3) *mâr* ^{d}*Adad-te-ia*

19 Note the dating of these tablets The agent of Bâbu-aḫ-iddina now listed under (2) is known as an ^{amêl}*ka-sir* (fuller), the contemporary of Ninurta-tukulti-Aššur is the *alaḫḫinu*

20 The reading of line 21 is not clear, but this is the best reconstruction on the basis of the seal (line 26)

21 Or, better, Aḫu-ṭâb

22 Even if the name of A-hi-ta-[bu] were to be restored in *KAJ* 21, 31, he would still not be the son of Šamaš-bêl-kitti, as Ebeling holds, but his father

S. v. Aḫu-tâbu (6) *and* (8)	*The references in both of these rubrics are to the same person.*
S. v. Aḫu-ṭâbu (7)	*Read S.* 98, 16, 44 *The suggestion to emend line 16 on the basis of line 44 seems valid.*
Page 15	
S. v. Âmur-dannûsa[23] (3) *and* (4)	*The references in both of these rubrics are possibly to the same person.*
S. v. Amurru-kitti-idi (2)	*Delete* = 1.[24]
Page 16	
S. v. Ana-pî-Ašur-lišlim	*Read* 190, 25, = ina-pî-Aššur-lišlim (274, 18).
Page 17	
S. v. Apapa (3), (4), (6), (7), (8), (9), (10)	*The references in all of these rubrics are to the same person.*[25]

Since, then, we have no reason to restore *KAJ* 21 on the basis of *KAJ* 20, 21, we propose to accept Ebeling's other suggestion (page 13), and to read *A-ḫi-da-iq* rather than to accept this unusual spelling of the name Aḫu-tâb

[23] Or, better, *Amur-dannûssa* (<—*dannût-sa*).

[24] *KAJ* 169 cannot be dated, and there is no basis for this identification of Ebeling's, or for the emendation of the only trace of the father's name from  to .

[25] a) The sons and grandsons of Apapa are all involved (except for rubric 8), either as debtors or as witnesses, in the transactions of Iddin-Kube and Kidin-Adad.

b) Only one Apapa appears personally in this general period of the reigns of Erîba-Adad and Aššur-uballiṭ (52, 1, 7), in the remaining cases, we deal with sons or grandsons of Apapa The name is thus not so common as it appears at first sight Beyond the man here identified, we know of an Apapa in the reign of Aššur-bêl-nišêšu (*KAJ* 172, 18, 19) and one, or possibly two, in the period of Adad-nirâri and Shalmaneser (98, 18, 56, 22)

c) In rubric 8, the land of the grandson of Apapa is sold not to Iddin-Kube, but to *Nûr-Kube mâr Bêlšunu* However, the land is in the same district (Puratati) as the land of a different son, which is transferred to Kidin-Adad (*KAJ* 160, 5 ff)

It seems probable, therefore, that this identification is to be made, and that *Apapa mâr Šamaš-iqîša* (*KAJ* 52, 1, 7) is the father or grandfather referred to in each of these rubrics

S. v. Apil-Adad	*Read, instead,* Aššur-ma-apla-eriš
S. v Aplia	*Delete* 283, 5, *for chronological reasons. Cf* Adad-aplija.
Page 18	
S. v. Arad-Ištar (2)[26]	*Omit* 225, 13; *and add as a separate entry, for chronological reasons* [27] *Delete* abarakku *following W.* 104, 8.
S. v. Arad-Ištar	*Add* (3) 101, 25 (?).
Page 19	
S. v. Arad-Kube (11)	*Perhaps the proper name of* 269, 12, *is to be read* Ku-be-nûr-ja *The surrounding context gives little clue for determining the word-division.*
S. v. Arad-Kube (12)	*Read* 92, 2, 6 *as a separate rubric, and add*: S. d. Da-ku-ra-si-i(?). *The remaining entries constitute a miscellaneous grouping.*
S. v. Arad-Šerua (1)	*Read, instead,* Mâr-Šerua (*see* Eigennamen, *page 60*).
S. v. Arad-Šerua (6)	*Add* 112, 11 (?), 245, 14, *S* 156, 11 (see Chapter III, note 57).
S. v Arad-Šerua (13)	*Add*=6.
S. v. Arad-Šerua (14) (*misc.*)	*Delete* 112, 11; 245, 14 (*see under rubric 6*). *Perhaps* 101, 25, *is to be read* Urad-Ištar.
S. v. Arad-Šerua (15)	*Perhaps to be read* Urad-Tešup (*see Chapter II, notes 31, 32*)
S. v Arad-Šerua	*Add* (16) V d I-di-ni-ja, 52, 6

[26] The reading adopted in this study, *Urad-Ištar*, was suggested by Lewy So, also, elsewhere for the sign *ERUM*

[27] To what extent one should identify the remaining bearers of this name who come from the time of Ninurta-tukulti-Aššur is uncertain In *KAJ* 203, 2, the *amêl urqi* cannot be the same as the *amêlabarakku* of the other tablets The *abarakku* of Ištar-tûra (*W* 96, 4) and the *abarakku* of *âlḪu-da-*[.] may or may not be identical The offerer of the *namurtu* of *W* 104, 8 may or may not be an *abarakku*. etc

Page 20

S. v. Arad-Tašmêtum (12)	*Remove* 35, 23, *and add to* (4) (HUCA *XXIV, p. 214*).
Add Arad-(*or* Urad-) Tešup	V. d. Šumu-lib-ši, 41, 18; 154, 23.
S v. Ardišešu	*Read* Arad-Tešup.
S. v. Asuat-Idigla (1) *and* (2)	*The references in both of these rubrics are to the same person* [28]
S. v. Ašur-[ ]	*Read* Aššur-dai̯i̯ân (*cf. Ebeling, page 26, s. v.* Ašur-mutakkil).

Page 21

S. v. Ašur-apla-ereš (1)	*Read* Aššur-ma-apla-eriš, *and add the reference* 244, 1, 5.
S. v. Ašur-bêl-[	*Read* Aššur-bêl-kâla (*not* –apli).

Page 22

S. v. Ašur-bêl-apli (2)	*Delete* " = 1."[29]
S. v. Ašur-bêl-ilâni (3)	*The identification of this man with the individual mentioned in S.* 19a, 9 *is improbable.*

[28] Ebeling's reading of *KAJ* 7 is based on a faulty reconstruction of the text Read.

(line 2) [*ᶠA-su-at*]-*ᵈIdigla mârat* [*Nir-bi-i̯a*] (line 3) [*ᵐIli-ma*]-*i-ri-ba urdu ša ᵐ*[*ᵈAmurru-na*]-*ṣir*

etc Both documents deal with the same transaction Ili-ma-erîba, the slave of Amurru-nâsir, has purchased Asuat-Idigla from Aššur-riṣui̯a In *KAJ* 7, Asuat-Idigla agrees to accept the duties of a wife of Ili-ma-erîba (lines 11 ff) and of a serf of Amurru-nâṣir (lines 20 ff) It is further stated that Amurru-nâṣir is in possession of the deed of transfer of Asuat-Idigla, by which her former owner acknowledges the receipt of her ransom (lines 30 ff) This document is, with little doubt, *KAJ* 167, bearing the seal of this former owner, Aššur-riṣui̯a (line 1) He states that in return for Asuat-Idigla (lines 2 f), he has received a Šubrian woman as her ransom, and that he accepts the responsibility of freeing Asuat-Idigla from claims of any third party (lines 15 ff.)

[29] *KAJ* 257 cannot be dated, but there is no evidence for identification of the Aššur-bêl-apli of line 15 with the man of the same name in rubric 1. The man referred to in *KAV* 201 is definitely excluded from such identification by chronological considerations

S. v. Ašur-bêl-kâla	*Add* 64, 26.
S. v. Ašur-bêl-uṣur (1) *and* (2)	*The references in both of these rubrics are to the same person.*
S. v. Ašur-bêl-uṣur (2)	*Remove* 197, 4 *and add under a separate heading.*[30]
S. v. Asur-dajân (*or* –dân) (1)	*Read* S. d. Ikkaru, limmu, 111, 20; *S.* 168, 24.
S. v. Ašur-dammeq (2)	*Delete* auch limmu, 262, 21.
S. v. Ašur-dammeq (4)	*Add* 262, 21.
Page 23	
S. v. Ašur-i(d)din(a) (7)	*Add* 229, 9! *Delete* 292, 17; *S* 135, rev. 10, *which are to be set under separate headings* (*Chapter III, note 34*).
Page 24	
S. v. Ašur-kîna-îdi	*The identification of the man mentioned in 6, 36 with the individua referred to in* S *212, 14 is likely; that he is also referred to in 143, 12 is possible on the basis of chronology, but positive evidence is lacking.*
Page 25	
S. v. Ašur-li'i (4)	*Delete.*[31]
S. v. Ašur-li'i (5) *and* (6)	*The references in both of these rubrics are to the same person.*
S. v. Ašur-ma-apla-ereš	*Add* (2) 144, 1, 5; 244, 1, 5 (*see above, Chapter III, notes 45–47*).
Page 26	
S. v. Ašur-mušêzib (5)	*Instead of* 9, 8, 24; *read* 98, 28. *Add* perhaps = (4).
S. v. Ašur-muštêpiš (1)	*Delete* 69, 22; *which is to be read* Aššur-pûti, *with Ebeling, page 27.*

30 In the documents other than *KAJ* 197, Aššur-bêl-uṣur brings a *namurtu* to the king. In *KAJ* 197, 4, a man of the same name receives a single animal from the royal supply Any identification of the two men is unlikely

31 Ebeling himself reads [*Me*]-*li*-[*saḫ*] (the son of Aššur-aḫ-iddina) See *Eigennamen*, page 61.

S. v. Ašur-muttabli	*Add* (2) S. d. Ki-di-Ku-be (tupšar.) 4, 30.
S. v Ašur-nâdin-šumišu	*We should expect* Aššur-šum-iddina (*cf line 14*).
Page 27	
S. v. Ašur-qarrad (2)	*Omit* 64, 24, *and set as a separate entry* (*see note 2*).
S. v. Ašur-rabi	*Add* (3) V. d. Bêl-qarrâd, limmu, 22, 25. = 1 (?).
Page 29	
S v. Ašur-zukupani (1)	*Delete* V d. (d)ba-bu-áḫ-iddina-(na).[32]
S. v. Ašur-zukupani (2)	*Add* = (1).[33]
S v. Ašur-zukupani (3)	*Delete* S. 135b, 9 (*see Chapter II, note 23*).
S v. Asusia (1) *and* (3)	*The references in both of these rubrics are to the same person.*[34]
S. v. Asusia	*Add* (7) 18, 6; 149, 9, *see note 1.*
Page 30	
S. v. Azunia (1)	*Delete, and read, instead,* = Azuzija (see note 1).
S v Bâbu-aḫ-iddina (1)	*Delete* *W.* 101, 18 *for chronological reasons.*

[32] Unless with Ebeling, we attribute two fathers to Bâbu-aḫ-iddina (cf s v Ibašši-ilu) Ebeling's false identification is based on *KAJ* 125, 4 ff , and by reason of it, he only tentatively identifies the Bâbu-aḫ-iddina of this tablet with the merchant known from numerous other sources (*Eigennamen*, page 30) However, *KAJ* 125, 4 ff is to be read

> (line 4) *ša* ^{md}*Ba-bu-aḫ-iddina*^{na} (line 5) [*ša qât*^{II}] ^{md}*A-šur-zu-kup-pa-ni*
> (line 6) [*i-na muḫḫi*] ^{md}*A-šur-mu-šab-ši*

[33] Note the appearance in this tablet of other subsidiaries of Bâbu-aḫ-iddina, namely Aššur-šallimani (lines 4, 10, 21) and Aššur-bêl-šallim (line 8)

[34] If the identification which we suggest is to be doubted, there is still no reason for Ebeling to identify the person mentioned in *KAJ* 100,6 with the father of Adad-risuja (line 34) rather than with the father of Damqat-Tašmete (line 5) However, it is natural that a daughter should be identified as being from the ^{âl}*dunni* of her father (lines 4–6) and also that a nephew of one of the principals should witness a transaction.

S v. Bâbu-aḫ-iddina (2)	*Perhaps add W*. 101, 18.
S. v. Bâbu-aḫ-iddina (3)	*There is no reason to doubt the reading or identification (see note 32).*
S. v. Bâbu-apal-uṣur (1) *and* (2)	*The references in both of these rubrics are probably to the same person. At least the references in* KAJ *178* and KAV *104 are to the same man.*

Page 31

After the reading Bêl[, *add the following entries* (cf. *Eigennamen, under the corresponding entry*):

Bêl-aḫ-eriš (Perh Bêl-šum-eriš)	S. d. Adadtuja 111, 15.
Bêl-aḫ-iddina	(1) S. d Adad-gugal 100, 25; (2) S. d Iddin-Marduk 128, 16.
Bêl-aḫḫêšu	(1) S. d Amur-dannûssa 150, 23; 152, 27; 153, 25; 155, 26; (2) S. d. Iddin-Kube mâr Rîš-Nabû 79, 12; (3) S. d. Kînija 67, 23; (4) E. d. Mâr-ûm-ešrê 152, 1, 8, (5) S. d. Apapa, V. d. Amurrija 98, 13; (6) V. d. Sîn-šadûni 164, 26, (7) 169, 24.
Bêl-âli	S. d. Adad-uballit 120, 27 [*or read, with Ebeling*, Iq(?)-zu(?)].
S. v. Bêl-ašared	*Add* (2) S. d. Šamaš-kîna-uṣur (*cf*. Eigennamen, *page 83*)

After the reading Bêl-bani *read the following entries*:

Bêlija	(1) V. d. Bur-šarru usw. 172, 2; 174, 4, 7, 10; (2) V. d. Kidin-Kube 86, 12, (3) *S*. 30, b 10.
Bêl-iqîša	215, 15
S v Bêl-lîṭer (1)	*Delete S*. 98, 5.

S. v. Bêl-lîṭer (2)	*Add S.* 98, 5. *Delete* "= 1."[35]
Page 32	
S. v. Bêl-nâdin-aḫḫê (2)	*Add* = (1) and (3).[36]
S. v. Bêl-naṣir (4)	*Read* V. d. Ili-eriš, = 6 (*Chapter II, note 39*).
S. v Bêl-qarrad (7)	*Delete* (= 8?). *The father is different and the chronology not suitable.*
Page 33	
S. v. [Bêl]-qarrad	*Add* (18) V. d. Adad-bêl-apli 88, 5.
S. v. Bêlšunu (1) *and* (2)	*The references in both of these rubrics are to the same person* (HUCA *XXIV, pp. 216 ff.*).
S. v. Bêlunu	*Add* (2) V. d. Baltu-kašid 71, 19 (*cf.* Eigennamen, *page 30*).[37]
S. v. Ber- [	*The identification of 55, 3, and 55, rev. 9 is uncertain.*
S. v. Ber-ilum	*Correct to* GV. d. Šu-Adad, 156, 6.
Page 34	
S. v. Ber-nâdin-aḫḫê (1)	*Add* 64, 3
S. v. Ber-nâdin-aḫḫê (2)	*Add* = (1) and (3).[38]

[35] It is not likely that the shepherd of Zêr-iqîša should be the agent (*amêlqîpu*) of Bâbu-aḫ-iddina

[36] Evidently *KAJ* 17, 1, 5, 17 all refer to the same Bêl-nâdin-aḫḫê By means of the transaction recorded in *KAJ* 17, Bêl-nâdin-aḫḫê (lines 1, 5) borrows lead from Kidin-Adad, as a pledge, he leaves his son, Iâkku-limmir (line 11) with the creditor. Thus the witness, *Iâkku-limmir mâr Bêl-nâdin-a-ḫi* (line 17) is evidently the son of the debtor.

[37] Ebeling records the name s. v. *Balṭu-kašid* as Belini, and apparently listed the name as such, so that it fell among the group of rubrics accidentally omitted from page 31 of his work However, the form seems to be the normal Assyrian genitive with vocal harmony of a nominative Bêlûnu Presumably, these forms are derived either from a nominative Bêlânum ("little lord"), or else from an original vocative, *Bêlâni* (cf. Lewy, *Orientalia*, XV, page 369, note 9) The form is then declined to give a nominative, *Bêlûnu*, etc For a similar example of vocalic harmony affecting a long vowel cf the name *Puhânu* (Stamm, page 301), which appears in these texts as (nominative) *Puḫûnu* and (genitive) *Puḫîni* (see Ebeling, *Eigennamen*, page 69).

[38] *KAJ* 162 deals with the disposition of land contracts which had been sealed by King Aššur-bêl-nišêšu. The Ber-nâdin-aḫḫê of the remaining tablets

S. v. Ber-šum-iddina (2) *and* (3)	*The references in both of these rubrics are to the same person.*[39]
Add [Be-i]r-tu-ri-uṣur	S. d. Kurbanu 116 RS. 6. *Cf. Eigennamen, s. v* Tu-ri-PAP.
S. v. Ber-uballiṭ (1) *and* (2)	*The references in both of these rubrics are probably to the same person.*
Page 35	
S. v. Bunia (4)	*225, 19=267, 20. 215, 25=239, 7. Other identifications doubtful. See also* 247, 6 (?).
Page 36	
S. v. Dajânia (1)	*Delete* auch 56, 1,5; *and list as a separate entry (see above, note 9).*
S. v. Daitte (3)	*Read* ᶠŠad-da-it-te (*cf.* W. *59, 4; and also* Eigennamen, *page* 80).
Add Da-ku-ra-si-i (?)	V. d. Urad-Kubi 92, 3.
Page 37	
S. v. Dugul-ila (1) *and* (2)	*The references in both of these rubrics are to the same person* (HUCA *XXIV, p. 191*).
S. v. Ea-iddina	*Add* 244, 7 (HUCA *XXIV, p. 251*).
S. v. Enlil-ašared (2)	*Omit.* (*Read* Bêl-qarrâd; *cf.* Eigennamen, *page 32*).
Page 38	
S. v. Enlilia (1)	*Delete* 293, 2, *and list as a separate entry.*
Page 39	
S. v. Erîba-Adad (2)	*Delete* 173, 12, *and add to (1).* W. *91 is, of course, excluded from such identification.*

is known to be a brother of the king (174, rev 10 f); and it is quite probable that his son should witness such a document as this

[39] Both tablets written in this eponymy year come from the period of Melisaḫ's activity

S. v. Erîba-Adad (3)	*Add* = (1). *Add likewise the references under Irîba-Adad,* Eigennamen, *page 50.*
Page 40	
S. v. Erîb-ilu (2) *and* (3)	*The references in both of these rubrics are probably to the same person.*
S. v. Erîb-ilu (11)	*The reason for Ebeling's comparison of 67, 6 and* S. *212, 4 at precisely this point is not clear.*
S. v. Erîb-Sin (1)	*Add* 35, 28 (HUCA *XXIV, pp. 212 f.*).
S. v. Eribtaiau (2) *and* (4)	*The references in both of these rubrics are probably to the same person.*
S. v. Erim-kîni	*The identification of 20, 25 with 142, 4 is uncertain.*
Page 41	
S. v. Girimaia	*Instead of* 1, 1, 9 *read* 91, 8.
Page 42	
S. v. Ḫimsateia	*Add* 302, 10 (?).
S. v. Iae	*Add* 70, 15, 4 (HUCA *XXIV, pp. 217 ff.*).
S. v. Iâku-limmer (4)	*Add* 36, 4.
Page 43	
S. v. Iasi	*Read* Ia̭e.
S. v. Ibašši-ilu (1)	*On* 82, 11 *and* 142, 23, *see Chapter II, note 12.*
S. v. Ibašši-ilu (3) *and* (14)	*To be identified.*[40] *Add also the Middle-Assyrian Votive Bead found at Tanis.*

[40] In rubric (3), Ibašši-ilu is the son of Ber-nâdin-aḫḫê, who is brother of King Aššur-bêl-nišêšu In rubric (14), the grandson of a certain Ibašši-ilu appears as *lîmu* (*KAJ* 10, 3). The documents in question (*KAJ* 10, *KAV* 212) come from the reigns of Aššur-uballiṭ and Adad-nirâri, which makes the lapse of time sufficient for the grandson of Ibašši-ilu to have become *lîmu* Moreover, in *KAV* 212, Aššur-uballit grants land to Rišêia, the son of Ibašši-ilu and father of the *lîmu* of *KAJ* 10, Kurbânu

S. v. Ibašši-ilu (6) — *For the possibility of adding* 142, 23, *see Chapter II, note 12.*

S. v. Ibašši-ilu (7) *and* (15) — *To be identified. Add, also, S.* 211, a7, b5; *and remove this reference from the miscellaneous listing, rubric (18).*

S. v. Ibašši-ilu (18) — *Delete* 174, 1 *cf. rubric (5); S.* 211, a7, b5 *cf rubric (7). Delete* 139, 8, 13, 19, *and add to rubric 5.*

S. v. Ibašši-ilu — *Add* (19) V. d. Šamaš-kitti-îdi(?), 49, 27.

Page 44

S. v. Iddin-Kube (1) *and* (3) — *Delete* E. d. mâr-ûmi-20-kam.[41] *Add* 35, 5, 66, 10, 22 *and delete from* (5) (*Chapter II, note 36*).

S. v. Iddin-Kube (2) *and* (4) — *The references in both of these rubrics are to the same person, as is shown by the enclitic* –ma *following the second mention of the name.*

S. v. Iddin-Kube (5) — *Perhaps the remaining tablets,* S. *127 and* S. *128 likewise refer to* Iddin-Kube mâr Rîš-Nabû.

S. v. Iddinni(a) (2) — *Delete* 263, 10 *for reasons of chronology (Chapter II, note 27).*

Page 45

S. v. Igaiau (2) *and* (3) — *The references in both of these rubrics are to the same person.*[42]

S. v. Igaiau (3) — *Omit* 64, 24 (*see note 2*).

S. v. Ikkaru — *Add* (2) V. d Aššur-da-a-an 111, 21.[43]

[41] The only tablet of Iddin-Kube which mentions *Mâr-ûmi-20*^{kam} is *KAJ* 60 *Mâr-ûmi-20*^{kam} is here the grandfather of the debtor, Laqîpu, and not of the creditor, Iddin-Kube (cf. *Eigennamen*, page 60)

[42] In both rubrics, the grandchildren of Igaiau borrow from Iddin-Kube

[43] Perhaps the phrase in question is to be read [*kunuk*] *Ik-ka-a-ri* rather than [*mâr*] *Ik-ka-a-ri*, although, in this case, the identity of Ikkaru would be undetermined

S. v. Ildat-kitti (1) *and* (2)	*The references in both of these rubrics are to the same person.*
S. v. Il-ittilu (1) *and* (2)	*The references in both of these rubrics are to the same person.*
S. v. Ilu-abi	*Add* (2) S. d. Ta-ri-ba-ti(?) 85, 25.

Page 46

S. v. Ilu-êreš (1)	*Add* 134, 20 (*Chapter II, note 39*).
S. v. Ilu-kidin-ilâni	*Read, instead,* Si(!)-qi-ilâni. *This alternate suggestion of Ebeling* (Eigennamen, *page* 77) *appears to be the better reading,* (*cf. line 12*).
Add [Ili-ma]?-abi	80, 27.

Page 47

S. v. Iluma-irîba (1) *and* (2)	*The references in both of these rubrics are to the same person.*
S. v. Ilu-malik (1) *and* (2)	*The references in both of these rubrics are to the same person.*[44]
S. v. Ilu-malik (3)	*Perhaps = the preceding.*
S. v. Ilu-nasḫira (1) *and* (2)	*The references in both of these rubrics are to the same person*[45]
S. v. Ilu-qarrad	*For chronological reasons, the men mentioned in these two references are not to be identified.*
S. v. Ilu-ša	*This reading seems extremely doubtful on the basis of Ebeling's copy of the text. Note also the extreme rarity of the theophorous element* DINGIR *in this period.*
S. v. Ilu-šêzibani (1)	*The men mentioned in the two references in this rubric are not necessarily the same individual.*

[44] The debtor's son as witness.

[45] In *KAJ* 20, Ili-nasḫira appears as the father of Pirḫija, who is indebted to Iddin-Kube In *KAJ* 146, Ili-nasḫira sells land to Iddin-Kube Moreover, the land which is sold is in the same district (Puraṭati) as the land which Pirḫija gave as security for his debt On the identity of Ili-nasḫira and Innasḫira, see *HUCA* XXIV, pp 212 f.

S. v. Ilu-šêzibani (2)	*Read* Aššur-šêzibani (*cf.* Eigennamen, *page 28*)
Page 48	
S. v. Ina-qibi-Ašur-lišlim	*Read* Ina-pî-Aššur-lišlim, = Ana-pî-Aššur-lišlim (q. v.). *Delete* 230, 14 (*see* Eigennamen, *page 70, s. v. Qibi-Ašur*).
S. v. Innamer	*Add* 35, 24 (HUCA *XXIV, p. 213*)
S. v. Innashira	*Not only to be derived from, but also = Ili-nasḫira, q. v.*
Page 49	
S. v. Iqîš-Adad (2) *and* (5)	*The references in both of these rubrics are possibly to the same person.*[46]
S. v. Iqîš-Adad (2)	*There is no reason to set* S. *26, b 14 in this rubric.*
S. v. Iqṣu (1)	*Read* Bêl-âli.
Page 50	
S. v. Iqṣu (3)	*Read* S. d. (*sic*) Adad-attadin (*cf.* Eigennamen, *page 7*).
S. v. Irîba-Adad	*All these references should be set under Erîba-Adad* (1), *with merely a cross-reference here.*
S. v. Ištar-ereš (3)	*Read* S d. Šulmânu-qarrâd, limmu, 124a, 23; S. 119, 18.[47]
S. v. Ištar-kidinni (2)	*The reading is doubtful. In any event, read:* V. d. a-ú-šá
Page 51	
S. v. Ištar-šum-ereš (2) *and* (3)	*The references in both of these rubrics are to the same person. See* Eigennamen, *page 12, s. v. Adad-teia.*

[46] The father is a scribe in the service of Aššur-aḫ-iddina (*KAJ* 62) and Melisaḫ (*KAJ* 114), and the son is a scribe in the service of Urad-Šerua (*KAJ* 62)

[47] Reading in *KAV* 119, 18.

. . . *mâr* ^{d}*Šul-ma-(nu!)-qarrâd*

S. v. Ištar-ummi	*The identity of the individuals mentioned in the two references is not established.*
S. v. Ittabši-dên-Ašur (1), (2) *and* (3)	*The references in all of these rubrics are to the same person.* (HUCA *XXIV, pp. 248, 263*).
Page 52	
S. v. Kidin-Adad (4)	*Add* = (1).
Page 53	
S. v. Kidin-Gula (2)	*Read* (2) 214, 14; 282, 12. (3) *S.* 99, 1, *S.* 100, 1; etc. (= 1) [48]
S. v. Kidin-ilâni (1)	*Delete* 262, 6; *which is to be added to* (*2*) (*see Chapter III, note 10*).
S. v. Kidin-Kube (2)	*Delete* 175, 44, *and add as a separate entry.*[49]
S. v. Kidin-Kube (6)	*Read* V. d. [A-šu]r-mu-tab-li, 4,31.
S. v. Kidin-Marduk (1)	*Delete* 7, 44 *and add to* (3). (*See note 28.*)
S. v. Kidinnia (3)	*The reading is doubtful.*
S. v. Kidin-Sin (1)	*Add* 275, 2! (*see note 18*).
Page 54	
S. v. Kidin-Sin (2)	*The reading in 130, 13 and its restoration on the basis of 142, 1, 3 are impossible for reasons of chronology.*
S. v. Kidin-Sin (7)	*Or else read* Šu-Sîn.
S. v. Kidin-Sin	*Add* (8) 246, 3.
Page 55	
S. v. Kizaia (1) *and* (2)	*The references in both of these rubrics are to the same person.*
S. v. Kubi-ereš (1) (4) *and* (8)	*The references in all of these rubrics are to the same person* (*Chapter II, note 11*).

[48] For chronological and other reasons. The Kidin-Gula of rubrics (1) and (3) now becomes one of the subsidiaries of Bâbu-aḫ-iddina. The Kidin-Gula of rubric (2) is a *bappiru* of the time of Ninurta-tukulti-Aššur

[49] The father of the scribe of *KAJ* 175 is given as [.]-Ku-bi.

Page 56

S. v. Kurbânu (3) — *The individual mentioned in 10, 2 is not to be identified with the man given in 10, 12, 14.*

S. v. Kurbânu (5) — *Read* V. d. Ber-tûri-uṣur(?).

S. v. Labunia (1), (2), (3), (4), *and* (5) — *The men referred to in all of these rubrics are to be identified* (HUCA *XXIV, pp. 195 ff.*).

S. v. Lâqîpu (5) — *Probably* = *(3)*.[50]

S v. Lara-Sin (1) *and* (2) — *The references in both of these rubrics are to the same person. See note 28.*

Page 57

S. v. Litt-ilu (1) *and* (2) — *The references in both of these rubrics are to the same person.*

S. v. Lullaiau (1) — *There is no evidence that* 215, 23 *belongs in this rubric.*

S. v. Lullaiau (5) *and* (6) — *The men referred to in each of these rubrics are to be identified. Ebeling's identification of the persons given in (6) and (7) likewise appears to be sound.*

Page 58

S. v. Mannu-gir-Ašur (3) *and* (4) — *Undoubtedly the men referred to in each of these rubrics are to be identified.*[51]

Page 59

S. v. Marduk-nâdin-aḫi (1) — *The persons given in the two references of this rubric cannot be identified for chronological reasons.*

S. v. Marduk-nirâri — *The readings are uncertain. No identification of the men given in the two references is possible.*

[50] The son of the debtor as witness.

[51] The debt owed by two men to Mannu-bal-Aššur is transferred by Mannu-bal-Aššur's son, presumably after the father's death, to Kidin-Adad. Why the son of a strange Mannu-bal-Aššur should be considered (line 9) is not apparent.

Page 60

S. v. Mâr-Idigla (8)	*Once again, the uncertainty of the date of* KAJ *215 prevents any possibility of identifying the men given in the two references.*
S. v. Mâr-Ištar (2)	*The person referred to in 36, 5 is not to be identified with the others. Note the differing traces of the father's name.*
S. v. Mâr-Šamaš (2), (3), *and* (4)	*The references in all of these rubrics are to the same person.*[52]
S. v Mâr-Šamaš (5)	*Add* = (2), (3), (4)?
S. v. Mâr-Šerua (12)	*To this miscellaneous rubric of otherwise unidentified persons add S.* 168, 4.

Page 62

S. v. Mudammeq-Marduk (2)	*Delete* 215, 28 *and* 239, RS. 3, 8; *and add as a separate entry.*
S. v. Mugabša	*Delete. Read* [A-šu]r-mu-tab-li, *q.v.*
S. v. Mukallimetu (1) *and* (2)	*The references in both of these rubrics are to the same person.*[53]
S. v. Mušabši (1) *and* (2)	*Or read* ᵈ[. . .] –mušabši.
S. v. Mušabši (3)	*Or read* Mu-šab-ši-u-[ᵈSibi] (*suggestion of Lewy*). *The reading* Šumu-libši *is also to be considered.*
S. v. Mušallim	*Perhaps* [Ilu-]šu-mušallim.
S. v. Mušallim-Adad (1)	*Add* 110, 30.
S. v. Mušallim-Ašur (4)	a) *Delete* 178, 11 *and add to rubric* (5). b) *Delete* 100, 30 (*See* Mušallim-Adad).

Page 63

S. v. Mušallim-Marduk	*Delete* "limmu? 110, 30?" *Cf. Mušallim-Adad.*

[52] Note the enclitic *–ma* after the second *Mâr-Šamaš* in *KAJ* 132, 5 On the remaining identifications, see *HUCA* XXIV, pp 191 f

[53] Brother of the creditor as witness

S. v. Mušêzib-Nergal (1) *and* (2)	*The references in both of these rubrics are to the same person.*
S. v. Mutaqqinu	*Read* V. d. Si-ku. (*Cf. Weidner,* Ass. Ep., *page 313*).

Page 64

S. v. Nabû-bêl-uṣur	*The identification of the men given in all three references is not certain.*
S. v Nadinu (3)	*Delete.*[54]

Page 65

S. v. Namru (1) *and* (2)	*The references in both of these rubrics are to the same person.*
S. v. Naqîdu	*Read* "Ad. S. d. Ki-ni-ia" *Cf.* Eigennamen, *page 54, where the relationship is correctly stated.*
S. v. Nasḫiria	*The references must, for reasons of chronology, be to two different men.*
S. v. Ninuaiau	*On the supposed identity of the persons referred to in all these references,* see *Chapter IV, notes 24, 26.*

Page 67

S v Nûr-Kube (1), (7), (8), (9), (12), (13)	*The references in all of these rubrics are to the same person* (HUCA *XXIV, pp. 216 ff.*).
S. v. Nûr-Kube (11)	*Perhaps the same as the above.*[55]

[54] Presumably Ebeling reads in *KAJ* 52:

(line 15) *a-na* ^{m}*I-din-Ku-bi mârl Na-di-n*[*u*]

However, the Iddin-Kube here involved as the creditor is evidently the man whose name is given in line 5 as the son of Rîš-Nabû The correct reading is therefore:

a-na ^{m}*I-din-Ku-bi i-na-di-i*[*n-nu*].

[55] The interpretation of this tablet is difficult With little doubt, the same Qîš-Amurru is referred to in lines 4 and 8 In line 4, he appears to be the son of Adad-šar, in lines 8 f, he is spoken of as the son of Nûr-Kube Any certain emendation, however, does not appear feasible on the basis of the tablets published so far.

S. v. Nusku-aḫ-iddina — *Read* V. d ᵈA-šur-ma-apla-êriš 144, 6; 244, 6 (HUCA *XXIV, p. 251*).

S. v. Nusku-ašared — *The men given in the references are not to be taken as identical.*

Page 68

S. v. Pauzi (1) *and* (2) — *The references in both of these rubrics are to the same person.*

Page 70

S. v. Qiš-Amurru (1) *and* (4) — *The references in both these rubrics are to the same person. In all probability, the individual referred to in* (3) *is also to be identified with the above. For a full discussion, see note 55.*

Page 71

S. v. Raggangia — *Read* ᶠGaggiḭa (Gangiḭa) — *Lewy.*

Page 72

S. v. Rêš-Nabû — *Perhaps* = (4).[56]

S. v. Rîmani-Adad (1) *and* (2) — *The references in both of these rubrics are probably to the same person.*[57]

Page 73

S. v. Sâmidu (2) *and* (3) — *The references in both these rubrics are possibly to the same person.*[58]

S. v. Sarniqu (1) *and* (4) — *The references in both these rubrics are to the same person.*[59]

[56] The function of Adad-pilaḫ in these tablets appears always to be that of witness to transactions of Kidin-Adad (*KAJ* 99, 163; 170) Thus he may well be his nephew.

[57] In these two contemporary tablets, the scribes are sons of Rîmanni-Adad.

[58] Note the role played by Melisaḫ in both tablets

[59] Note the following reconstruction of *KAV* 211:

(line 7) *ša iš-tu* ᵐ*Ibašši-ilu* (line 8) *ù* [*Sa*]-*ar*-[*ni-qi*] (line 9) [*mârê* ᵈ*Šamaš-ši-me ilqi* . .] (line 13) ᵐ*Ibašši-ilu* (line 14) *ù* ᵐ*Sa-ar-ni-qi* . (cf *KAJ* 170).

Both tablets deal with the carpenter who is sold by these two brothers to Kidin-Adad.

S. v. Sîku	Read S. d. Mu-ta-qi-ni (Weidner, Ass. Ep., page 313).
Add Siḫi	V. d. Girimaja und Tabbini 91, 9.
Page 74	
S. v. Simteia	Read Adad-te-ja [^{d}(!)Im-te-ja]. Cf. on Kidın-Sın.
S. v. Sin-[	The men given in the two references are not, of course, to be identified.
S. v. Sın-dajân (4) and (5)	The men given in the two rubrics are not to be identified. See s. v. Kidin-Sin.
Page 75	
S. v. Sin-dajan (5) and (6)	The references in both these rubrics are to the same person.[60]
S. v. Sın-mešê	Read Sîn-še-me-e (suggestion of Lewy).
Add Sın(?)-mudammiq	V. d. Mâr-ûmi-20^{kan} 44, 17.
Page 76	
S. v. Sin-naṣir (1)	Since 79 = 166, read 79, 9, 15, 18.
S. v. Sin-nasir (3) and (4)	The references in both these rubrics are to the same person. Cf. Eigennamen, page 30, s. v. "baltu-ıtti̇a" and "balṭu-kašid."
S. v. Sin-naṣir (6)	Delete 79, 1 and add to rubric 1. Delete 166, 1.
S. v. Sinnia (5) and (6)	The references in both these rubrics are possibly to the same person.[61]
Page 77	
S. v. Sin-šeia (1)	Delete 310, 31, and add as a separate rubric.
Add Sin-šemê	See Sın-mešê for details.
S. v. Sin-uballiṭ	Add (7) lîmu, 77, 23(?).
S. v. Sîqi-ilâni (1) and (3)	The references in both these rubrics are to the same person.

[60] The brothers of the creditor as witness
[61] The son of the debtor as witness

Page 78	
S. v. Ṣâbê-Ištar (1) *and* (2)	*The references in both these rubrics are to the same person.*
S v. Ṣâbê-Ištar (1)	*Read* V. d. A-bu-ṭâb (*Cf.* Eigennamen, *page 6*).
S v. Ṣillia (2)	*Read* S d. Enlil-bani (ibid. *page 38*).
Page 79	
S. v. Ṣilli-Kube (8)	*The men given in these two references are not to be identified.*
Page 80	
S. v. Ṣilli-Marduk (3)	*Reading extremely doubtful Read* S. d. [. . . .]-ku-ki-i̯a. *Perhaps the name itself is to be read* [. . . .]-šir-^{d}Marduk.
S. v. Ša-Adad-nînu	*There is no connection between the two references.*
S. v. Šaddaittu (1), (2) *and* (3)	*The individuals referred to in all of these rubrics are to be identified, as Ebeling, no doubt, intended.*
S. v. Šâkin-sumê (2) *and* (3)	*The references in both these rubrics are to the same person.*[62]
Page 81	
S. v. Šamaš-âmeri (1)	*Delete* 154, 1.[63]
S v. Šamaš-âmeri (1) *and* (2)	*The references in both these rubrics are to the same person.*[64]
S. v. Šamaš-amranni	*Chronology excludes the possibility of this reading in 159, 4.*
Page 82	
S. v. Šamaš-dajân (3)	*Delete*=1. *Reconstruction on the basis of rubric (1) is excluded for reasons of chronology. Add*=(2) (*Chapter II, note 33*).

[62] Two of his grandsons would then figure as witnesses in documents of Melisaḫ (*KAJ* 73, 17 ff.; *KAJ* 95, 15 ff)

[63] Which must be read *^{md}Šamaš-[še-zi-ib]*, the seller of the land (cf line 9, cf also, *Eigennamen*, page 85)

[64] A son is given to the father's brother for adoption

S. v. Šamaš-iddin	*Read* Aššur-iddin, *q. v*
S. v. Šamaš-ilušu?	*Read* Šamaš-tukulti.
S. v. Šamaš-ılu-ašaridu	*Add* (3) tupšarru 74, 5.
Page 83	
S. v. Šamaš-kîmuia	*Read* Perhaps = Šamaš-kîmu-abija (HUCA *XXIV, p. 252*).
S. v. Šamaš-kîna-uṣur (2)	*Delete* 252, 2 *and add as a separate entry.*
S. v. Šamaš-kitti-îdi (1)	*Add* 59, 24.[65]
Page 84	
S. v. Šamaš-mušêzib	*Add* (8) V. d. Erib-ili 26, 21(?).
S. v. Šamaš-pa[	*Read* Šamaš-tukulti.
Page 85	
S. v. Šamaš-šêzib (2) *and* (3)	*Perhaps the references in both these rubrıcs are to the same person.*
Page 86	
S. v. Šamaš-šumu-lîšir	*Read* Ilu-amuqa, *cf. Ebelıng, page 45.*
S. v. Šamaš-tukulti (2)	*Add* 70, 1, 5 (HUCA *XXIV, pp. 217 f.*).
S. v. Šamaš-tûra-lîšir (1) *and* (2)	*The references ın both these rubrıcs are to the same person.*[66]
S v. Šamaš-uballiṭ (2)	*Add* [150, 20]?
S. v. Šamaš-uballiṭ (4)	*Add* 153, 24.
Page 87	
Add Šu-ᵈAdad	E. d. Be-ir-ili 156, 5, 14, 18.
Add [Šu?]-Ištar	47, 6 (*See Taklâku-ana-Marduk*).
Add Šilmi-Tešup	S. 30, 17
S. v. Šulma-ašared	*Delete S.* 119, 18 (*See s. v. Šulmânu-qarrad*).
S. v. Šulmânu-qarrad (1) *and* (2)	*The evıdence for identıficatıon of the men referred to ın these two rubrics is not compellıng.*

[65] Possıbly, also, read: *S d Ibašši-ılu*

[66] Though the dating of the tablets ın question is doubtful, it ıs evident that, on the whole, the same names are repeated in each

S. v. Šulmânu-qarrad (3)	*Add S* 119, 18.
Page 88	
S. v. Šumma-Adad	179, 23, 24 *should be listed as a separate rubric.*
S. v. Šummi-Tešup	*The reason for this reading in b. 8 is not clear.*
S. v. Šumu-libši (2) *and* (3)	*Read, perhaps,* S. d. Arad-Tešup (ar-di-Te-šup).
S. v. Šumu-libši (8)	*Delete* 132, 25, *and add to rubric (1). The individuals given in the remaining two references should not be identified. Perhaps* 91, 5 *may be Mušabšiu-[Sibi], q. v.*
S. v. Šunu-qardu	*The first reference may, conceivably, be to a different person.*
S. v. Šuprîtu (1)	*Delete* 170, 4(?) *and add to* (2).
Page 89	
S. v. Sururia (1)	*Delete* V. d. Arad-ku-bi? *Read, instead,* V. d. In-na-me-ir, = (2) (HUCA *XXIV, p. 213*).
S. v. Šururia (2)	*Add* = (1).
S v Taklâku-ana-Marduk	*Perhaps, the son's name is to be read:* Šu-Ištar.
S v. Tarîbatu? (3)	*Read* Admati-ili (*cf.* Eigennamen, *page 13*).
Page 90	
S v. Tukulti-Adad (1) *and* (2)	*Both references are, of course, to the same man.*
S. v. Turi-PAP	*Read* Ber-tûri-uṣur (*q. v.*).
Page 91	
S. v. Ṭâb-Ašur (2)	*Omit* "= 1." *Add* "Or perhaps read Ṭâb-Ištar, see 85, 30."
S v. Ṭâbiae	*Perhaps read* Ṭâb-a-[ḫu]?
S. v. Ṭâbini	*The text of 92, 8 is very doubtful. Even accepting Ebeling's reading, there is no reason for identifying the persons given in the two references.*

S. v. Ṭâb-ṣilli-Šamaš (1) — *Read* Ṭâb-ṣilli-Aššur.[67]

Page 92

S. v. Ubâria (2) — *Evidently* = (1) and (3).

S. v. Ubazuia — *In 18, 1, a reference to the seal of the debtor is needed, and thus it might be necessary to read* U-ba-ri!-ia.[68]

S. v Upru (3) — *Add* 218, 4; 318, 4; *which are to be deleted from rubric* (7). *Add* = (6)? (HUCA *XXIV, p. 249*).

S. v. Upru (6) —
a) S. *19, a7 is doubtful. The date of* S. *19 is still undetermined, nor is its nature as a lîmu-list at all likely.*[69]
b) *Delete S.* 167, 10, *which is to be read* Upru- [Aššur] *q. v.*
c) *Add* 138, 3 [70]
d) *Add* 240, 2, 11.[71]

S. v. Upru (7) — *Delete the last two references, as indicated s. v.* (3).

S. v. Upru (8) — *Delete* 240, 2, 11, *as explained above.*

[67] Cf line 19, written over an erasure. Apparently the name was written ncorrectly at first, and corrected only in one place.

[68] On the other hand, the witness, Iddin-Bêl may very easily be the son of the creditor. In that case, we should have to explain the following variants of the same name in *KAJ* 18:

(line 11) *Ú-ba-* 

(lines 5 and 14) *Ú-ba-* 

(line 21) *Ú-ba-*  (Read U-ba-si!-ia)

Perhaps all were means of reproducing the same foreign sound in Akkadian

[69] Cf. Weidner, *AfO* XIII, page 111, note 10.

[70] Read in *KAJ* 138, on the basis of the later mention of the eponymy of Tukulti-Ninurta:

(line 2) *ša li-me* (line 3) [*Up-r*]*i*

[71] The omission by Ebeling is again the result only of oversight. Ebeling saw the restoration of Upru in line 11 (cf. rubric 8), where the reading is:

ša li-me U[*p-ri*]

Note also lines 1 f.

(line 1) *ša l*[*i-me*] (line 2) *m Up-ri* (cf. line 4)

Page 93

Add Urṣu — S. d. Sîn-šar-ilâni 168, 19 (*cf.* Eigennamen, *page 76*).

S. v. Uṣur-kînu (3) — *Read* = 1, *rather than* s 1.[72]

S. v. Uzê — *Add* 70, 6 (HUCA *XXIV*, pp. 217 f.).

[72] The only difference being the customary use of the genitive after ***kunuk*** and of the nominative after *maḫar* ().

TABLE VII

The Principal Merchants & Officials of the Middle-Assyrian Business & Juridical Documents

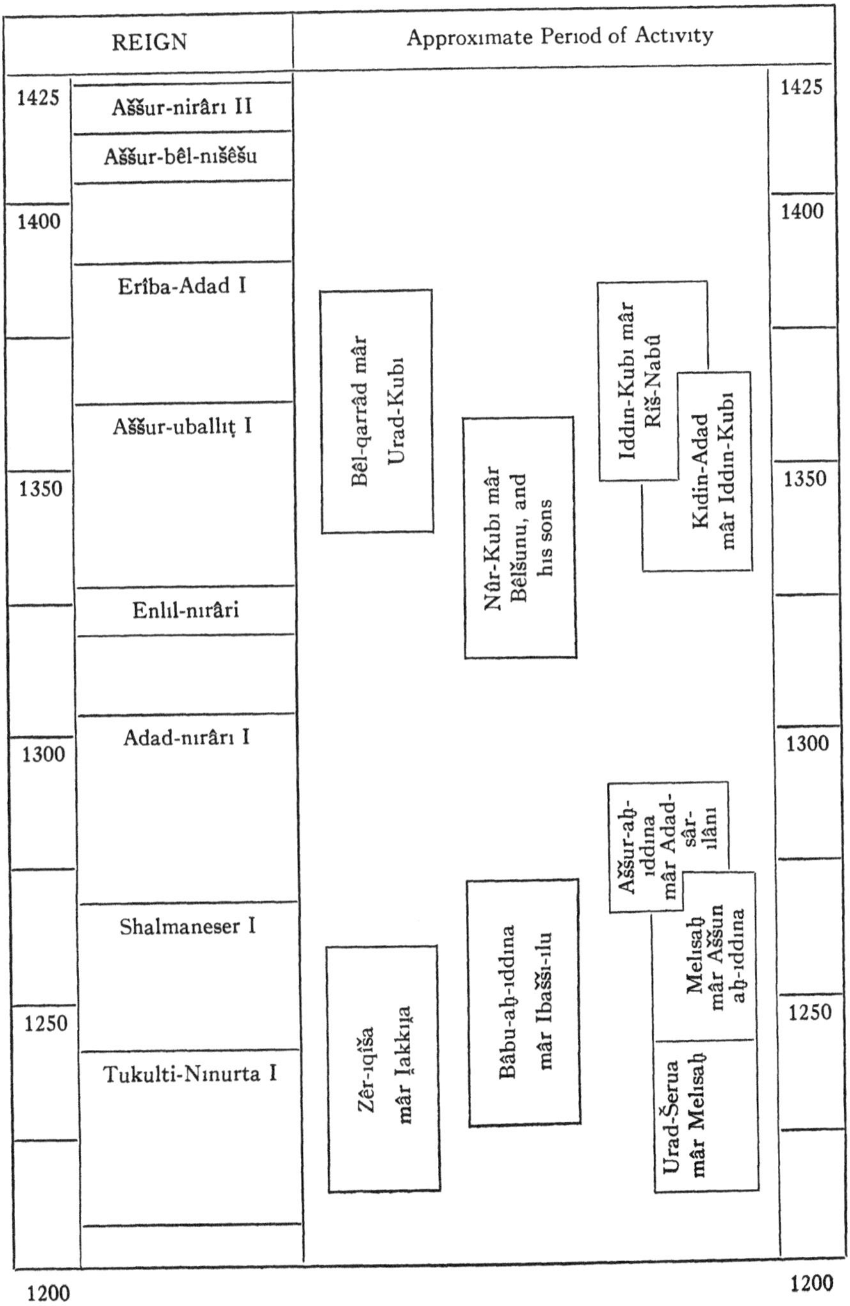

INDEX OF TEXTS DATED AND DISCUSSED[1]

Assur 6045f: 243 n. 31
Assur 9819: 202 f, 214 n 37, 230 n 6, **247**, 248 ff., 255 n. 52, 257 n 59, n 62, 259 n 64, 263, II 114 n. 24
Assur 11017g. **246**
Assur 11017n: **245**
Assur 11017w: **244**
Assur 11018m. **244**
Assur 11018o: **245**
Assur 11018z **244**
Assur 12758· II 107 n 3, **113**, 123
Assur 13058. II 107 n 2, n 3, 110 n. 18, **113**
Assur 14410p: 236

Bi 5: **234 f.**, 270
Bi 6: **234 f.**
Bi 8· 231, **234 f.**, 269
Bi 9: **234 f.**, 268
Bi 13: 229, **234 f.**, 267
Bi 15. **234 f.**, 265
Bi 25. **234 f.**, 270
Bi 31: 229, **234 f.**, 270
Bi 38: **234 f.**, 266
Bi 40: **234 f.**, 265
Bi 91. **234 f.**, 265

CT XXXIII 14b: **235**, 266, II 124 n. 26
CT XXXIII 15b **208**, 227

KAH I 3 II 124 n 30
KAH I 5: 228, 231 n 9, II 125 n 32
KAH I 13· 230, II 123 n 20, 125 n 33
KAH I 15: 231
KAH I 63: II 119 n 4
KAH II 20: II 133 n. 66
KAH II 27: 199, II 119 n. 4
KAH II 28. II 119 n. 4
KAH II 29. II 124 n. 30
KAH II 33: 228
KAH II 34: 228, II 133 n 66
KAH II 35: II 124 n 30
KAH II 41 234
KAH II 42: II 133 n 66
KAH II 48–50· II 133 n 66
KAH II 52: II 133 n 66
KAH II 54· II 124 n 30
KAH II 58· 241 n. 27, II 124 n. 30
KAH II 60: 241 n 27, II 124 n 30
KAH II 61. 241 n. 27, II 125 n 33
KAH II 84: II 123 n 20
KAJ 1: **197 f.**, 210, 219, 224
KAJ 2. 221, **223**, 227
KAJ 6 **203**, 212, 219 f, 226
KAJ 7. II 120 n 6
KAJ 8. 190 n 7, **203 f.**, 226, II 123 n 25
KAJ 10· 203 f, **235**, 261 n 74, 265, II 110 n 18, 122 n 13
KAJ 11. **204**, 205 f, 221, 226
KAJ 12: 195 n 5, **201 f.**, **207**, 208, 221, 222 n 44, 226, II 121 n 9
KAJ 13. **199**, 200 f, 209, 221 f, 225, II 121 n. 11, 126 n 39
KAJ 14· 194 f, **198**, 221, 224, 254 n 51
KAJ 15· **243 ff.**, 271
KAJ 16. **215**, 225
KAJ 17: 199 n 8, **200 f.**, 215, 221 f, 225
KAJ 18: **199**, 221, 222 n 44, 225
KAJ 19· **200 f.**, 221 f, 225
KAJ 20. **194**, 198, 201 n 12, 221, 222 n 44, 224
KAJ 21. 211 n 34, **220**, 227
KAJ 22 **192**, 193
KAJ 23: 195 n 4, **209**, 226

[1] Passages which discuss the dating of a specific text are indicated by bold face type. References to Part II of these studies (*HUCA* XXV, pp. 107–162, above) are preceded by II Otherwise, Part I (*HUCA* XXIV, pp 187–273) is intended

KAJ 24: **209**, 226, II 121 n 9, 126 n. 38, 128 n 48
KAJ 25: **197 f.**, 206 n 22, 218 f, 224
KAJ 26: **201 f.**, 206, **207**, 221, 222 n. 44, 226, 243 n 35, 255 n 55
KAJ 27. **199**, 208, 225
KAJ 28. 206 f, **209**, 216, 219, 226
KAJ 29· 195 n 5, **205**, 207, 221, 222 n 44, 223 n 45, 226
KAJ 30 **243**, 245 f, 250, 252, 272
KAJ 33 214, **215**, 225
KAJ 34. 214, **215**, 216, 225
KAJ 35. **212**, 214, 221, 222 n 44, 225, II 121 n 9
KAJ 36: **199**, 203, 210 f, 217 n 41, 220, 226
KAJ 37: 192 n 10
KAJ 38: **214**, 225
KAJ 41: **210 f.**, 214 ff, 226, II 121 n 9
KAJ 42 **222**, 225
KAJ 43· 214, **215**, 225
KAJ 45: **216**, 225
KAJ 47. II 131
KAJ 48 **236**, 237, 256, 270
KAJ 49: **237**, 256, 270
KAJ 50: **192**, 193
KAJ 51: **231**, 233, 255, 269
KAJ 52· **197 f.**, 221, 224
KAJ 53: **205 f.**, 207, 221, 223, 226
KAJ 54. **255**, 262 n 75, 266
KAJ 56. 245 f, **255**, 258 n 63, 266
KAJ 58· **209**, 210, 216 f, 219, 225
KAJ 59: **237**, 250, 252, 270
KAJ 60: **199**, 204 ff, 221, 222 n 44, 225
KAJ 61: 195, **208**, 221, 223, 227
KAJ 62: **230**, 254, 268, II 127
KAJ 63. **201 f.**, **207**, 221, 222 n 44, 223, 226, II 121 n 9
KAJ 64 190 n 7, **195**, 198, 205, 224
KAJ 65. **209**, 226
KAJ 66: 214 n 36, **222**, 225
KAJ 67: **205**, 221, 223, 227
KAJ 68 (=*KAJ* 64)
KAJ 69: 211 n 32
KAJ 70 **211**, 216 ff, 227
KAJ 72 **255**, 269, II 129 n 51
KAJ 73. **255**, 269
KAJ 75. **229 f.**, 254, 266 f, II 122 n 16
KAJ 76. **255**, 258, 266
KAJ 79: **208**, 221, 223, 227
KAJ 80: **232**, 233, 237, 256, 270
KAJ 81. **255**, **258**, 268
KAJ 82· 201 f n 12
KAJ 83. 230 n 8, **231**, 232, 237, 254, 256 n 58, 268, II 124 n 27
KAJ 85: 192 n 10
KAJ 86. **205**, 227
KAJ 88. 202, **249**, 271
KAJ 89· 245 f, **255**, 267, II 122 n 16
KAJ 90. **231**, 255, 269
KAJ 92: II **113 f.**
KAJ 93. **243 ff.**, 248, 250, 271, II 129 n 51
KAJ 94: **256**, 269
KAJ 95: 211 n. 33, **256**, 269
KAJ 96: **207**, 211 n 33, 227
KAJ 97 **250**, 271
KAJ 98. 254 n 51, **255**, 266, II 127
KAJ 99: **199**, 209, 221, 223, 225
KAJ 100· **255**, 266
KAJ 101. II **114**
KAJ 102. **256**, 269, II 122 n 14
KAJ 103: 233 n 15, **241**, 248, 273, II 122
KAJ 104. **236**, 270
KAJ 106: 233 n 15, **241**, 248, 273, II 110 n 18, 122
KAJ 107: **242**, 248, 273
KAJ 108: 242, **256**, 258, 268
KAJ 109: 230 n. 8, **231**, 233, 235, 253, 255 f., 268
KAJ 110. 230 n 8, **239 f.**, 257, 272, II 129
KAJ 111: **240 f.**, 247 f, 253, 257, 273
KAJ 112 **257**, 259, 271
KAJ 113 230, **231**, 233, 253, 256, 268
KAJ 114 **230**, 233, 255, 268

KAJ 115 **232**, 256, 270
KAJ 116 202 f., **241**, 249, 253, 257, 273
KAJ 117 (=*KAJ* 107)
KAJ 118: **256**, 258, 268
KAJ 119 **230**, 232, 237, 255, 268
KAJ 120 **256**, 258, 268, II 124 n 27
KAJ 121: **233**, 253, 255, 269
KAJ 122. **239 f.**, 257, 272
KAJ 123: **231**, 254 n 51, 259 ff., 267
KAJ 124. **236**, 256 n 57, 270
KAJ 124a. 229 n 4, **235**, 270, II 122 n. 13
KAJ 125: **236**, 259 ff., 270
KAJ 126: II **115**, 123
KAJ 127. 250, **253**, 271
KAJ 128 238 n 21, **240 f.**, 257, 273
KAJ 129 II **114 f.**, 123
KAJ 130 253, 254 n 51, **255**, 266
KAJ 131: II **111**
KAJ 132 **191 f.**, 193
KAJ 133: 233 n 15, **241**, 242, 248, 273
KAJ 134 **215**, 225, II 127
KAJ 135: **211**, 227
KAJ 137 **255**, 266, II 122 n 14, n 15
KAJ 138: **237 ff.**, 272
KAJ 139 **191 f.**, 193
KAJ 140: 189 n 2
KAJ 142 201 n 12, **208**, 226
KAJ 143: **212**, 227, II 123 n 25
KAJ 144. **238 ff.**, 250 ff., 272
KAJ 145: **228**, 253 f., 265, II 124 n 27
KAJ 146: **212 ff.**, 221, 225, II 121 n 9
KAJ 147 **195 ff.**, 224
KAJ 148. **198**, 224, 254 n 51
KAJ 149: **201 f.**, **207**, 208, 221, 222 n 44, 223, 226
KAJ 150. 205 n 20, **206 f.**, 210, 220 f., 227, 243 n 34, 250
KAJ 151: 197 f., **206 f.**, 209, 219, 227
KAJ 152 **201 f.**, **207**, 211, 216 f., 226
KAJ 153. 197 f., **205 f.**, 210 n 30, 211, 216 ff., 226
KAJ 154: 198, **210**, 211, 216 f., 219, 227, II 121 n 9
KAJ 155. 197 f., **205 f.**, 210 n 30, 211, 216 ff., 226
KAJ 156: **214**, 227
KAJ 157. **208**, 221, 227, 228 n 2, II 126 n 39
KAJ 158 **232**, 259 ff., 270, II 122 n 13
KAJ 159 **232**, 260 f., 270, II 122 n 16
KAJ 160 **194**, 222, 224
KAJ 161. 195 ff., **199**, 200 f., 209, 221, 223, 225
KAJ 162: **190**, 192 f., II 120, 123 n 25
KAJ 163. 195 ff., 208 n 26, **209**, 221, 223, 226
KAJ 164: **200 f.**, 208, 225
KAJ 165: **206 f.**, 221, 227, 243 n 64, 250, II 121 n 10, 126 n 41, 129
KAJ 166 (=*KAJ* 79)
KAJ 168 202, **249**, 271, II 122 n 14
KAJ 170 **199 f.**, 201, 221, 223, 225, II 121 n 10
KAJ 171. **233**, 247, 268
KAJ 172. **190**, 193, 200 n 11, II 123 n 25
KAJ 173 **199**, 226
KAJ 174: **190**, 191 ff
KAJ 175 200 n 11, **208**, 227, II 126 n 38
KAJ 176. **197 f.**, 224
KAJ 177: **189 f.**, 193
KAJ 178 **259**, 260 ff., 271
KAJ 179: **198**, 221 f., 224
KAJ 180: **240**, 272
KAJ 182: **233**, 270
KAJ 183 **194**, 224
KAJ 184. **233**, 270
KAJ 185: II **111**, 114 n 24, 123 n 21
KAJ 186: II **111**

KAJ 187. II **111**, 123
KAJ 188. II **111**
KAJ 189: II **111**, 123 n 21
KAJ 190. **264**, 274
KAJ 191. II **111**
KAJ 192: II **111**, 115, 123 n 19, n 21
KAJ 193: II **111**
KAJ 194–195: II **112**
KAJ 196. 189 n 2
KAJ 197: II **111**
KAJ 198–204: II **112**
KAJ 205· II **112**, 114 f
KAJ 206–208. II **112**
KAJ 209. II **112**, 123 n 19
KAJ 210· II **112**
KAJ 211. II **112**, 114
KAJ 212: 257 n 61, II **112**
KAJ 213: II **112**
KAJ 214: II **112**, 114 n 24
KAJ 216· II **112**
KAJ 217: **236**, 260 f , 270, II 124 n 27
KAJ 218: 202 f , **249**, 271
KAJ 219: **235**, 270
KAJ 221–222 II **112**
KAJ 223· **236**, 256 n 57, 270
KAJ 225: **232**, 233, 270
KAJ 227: **258**, 266
KAJ 228: **243 ff.**, 271
KAJ 229: **206 f.**, 223, 227, 250
KAJ 230. 238 f , **240**, 250, 252, 253 n 48, 264 n. 77, 272
KAJ 232: **258**, 266
KAJ 233: 228 n 1
KAJ 235· II **112**
KAJ 237: II **111**, 112 n 21, 123
KAJ 238 **238 ff.**, 250, 252, 272
KAJ 240: 237 f , **239 f.**, 263, 272
KAJ 241: **239 f.**, 250 ff , 272
KAJ 242: **230**, 247, 250, 260 f , 268
KAJ 244 238, **239 f.**, 250 ff , 272, II 127
KAJ 245: **257**, 259, 271, II 122 n 12
KAJ 250. 211 n 33
KAJ 251 228 n 2, II 126 n 39
KAJ 253. 223 n 45, 231 n 9, **259** 269
KAJ 254. II **112**
KAJ 255: **243**, 273, II 122 n 15
KAJ 256. 260, **263**, 274
KAJ 257. 243 n 35
KAJ 258 231 n 9, **259**, 269
KAJ 259: II **115**
KAJ 262. **231**, 254, 267
KAJ 263. 208 n. 27, **249**, 271
KAJ 264. II **112**, 114 n 24, 123
KAJ 265 II **112**, 113
KAJ 267. **232**, 270
KAJ 268. **257**, 259, 271
KAJ 269 223 n 45
KAJ 270. 189 n. 2
KAJ 271. 250, **253**, 271
KAJ 272: **238 ff.**, 272
KAJ 274. 260, **263**, 264, 274
KAJ 275: **233**, 268, II 122 n. 16
KAJ 278: II **112**
KAJ 279· 248, 260, **263**, 271
KAJ 280· II **112**
KAJ 281: II **111**, 123
KAJ 282: II 111, **112**, 114 n 24, 115
KAJ 283. II **112**
KAJ 284: II **113**, 115
KAJ 285: 189 n. 2
KAJ 286 II **113**
KAJ 287. 189 n 2
KAJ 288: II **113**
KAJ 289. **240**, 272
KAJ 290. **230**, 268
KAJ 291: **240**, 243 f , 272
KAJ 292 **243 ff.**, 250, 271
KAJ 293· **243 ff.**, 271
KAJ 293a: 260, **263**, 271
KAJ 294. **215**, 225
KAJ 301: **242 f.**, 244, 272
KAJ 302. II **115**
KAJ 306: 260, **263**, 274
KAJ 307. **228**, 265
KAJ 308. **232**, 270, II 124 n 27
KAJ 310· 211 n 33, **236**, 270
KAJ 311 **232**, 270
KAJ 312· **237 ff.**, 272
KAJ 313: **243 ff.**, 271

KAJ 314: 215, **236 f.**, 243, 246, 270
KAJ 315 **256**, 259, 269
KAJ 316: **243 ff.**, 267, 272
KAJ 318· 202 f., **249**, 271
KAJ 319. **242**, 248, 273
KAV 93: **194**, 224
KAV 96: **228**, 260 f, 265, II 126 n 39
KAV 97: II 127 n 44
KAV 98. **236**, 253 n 48, 260 f, 270
KAV 99: 248, 260, **263**, 271
KAV 100: 253 n 48, 260, **263**, 274
KAV 102: 257 n 61, **259**, 260 ff, 271
KAV 103: **232**, 260 ff., 270
KAV 104: **236**, 260 ff., 270
KAV 105: 257 n. 61, **259**, 261 f, 271
KAV 106: **240**, 261 ff, 272
KAV 107: **228**, 261, 265
KAV 108: 261, **263**, 274
KAV 109 **259**, 261 f., 271
KAV 110· **258**, 266
KAV 111: **258**, 266, II 131 n 58
KAV 119. 229 n 4, **235**, 270
KAV 135: 207 n 23, 240 n 24, 243 n. 64
KAV 156. **236**, 256, 270
KAV 157: **258**, 266
KAV 158· **258**, 266
KAV 159: II **115**
KAV 160: 240 n 24
KAV 167 240 n 24
KAV 168 211 n. 33, **240 f.**, 243 f, 273
KAV 169 238 n 21, **240 f.**, 243 f, 273
KAV 194: **228**, 261, 265
KAV 196: **238 ff.**, 261 f., 272
KAV 200· **240**, 261 f, 272
KAV 201: **243 ff.**, 248, 271 f
KAV 203. **232**, 261 ff, 270
KAV 205: 248, 261, **263**, 271
KAV 207. 228 n 1
KAV 209: **195**, 200 n. 10, 214 f, 224, II 120
KAV 210 (=*KAJ* 173)
KAV 211. **199**, 200 f, 221, 223, 225, II 121 n 10
KAV 212: **203**, 212, 226, 235
KAV 217: **263**, 271
KUB IV, 93: 199 ff.

Speleers 314: **233**, 268

VAT 8722: II 127
VAT 9363: II 107 n. 3, **113**
VAT 9378· II 107 n 3, **113**
VAT 9405. II 107 n 3, **113**
VAT 16380 (=*Assur* 9819)
VAT 16381: 246, II 114 n 24

W. 50: II 107 n. 1, 111, **113**
W. 51–54: II 107 n 1, **111**
W 55–62: II **107** n 1, **113**
W 63: II 107 n 1, **113**, 123 n 19
W. 64–71: II 107 n. 1, **113**
W 72· II 107 n. 1, **113**, 127
W. 73–75: II 107 n 1, **113**
W 76: II 107 n 1, **113**, 134 n 67
W. 77· II 107 n 1, **113**
W 78: II 107 n 1, 112 n 21, **113**, 114 n. 24
W. 79: II 107 n 1, **113**
W. 80 II 107 n. 1, **113**, 123 n 19
W. 81–88: II 107 n. 1, **113**
W. 89· II 107 n 1, **113**, 134 n 68
W 90. II 107 n 1, **113**, 123 n 22
W 91–97: II 107 n 1, **113**
W. 98: II 107 n 1, 108, **113**
W. 99: II 107 n 1, **113**
W 100. II 107 n 1, **113**, 123, 127
W 101: II 107 n 1, **113**, 114 n 24
W 102. II 107 n 1, **113**, 123
W. 103: II 107 n 1, **113**, 123 n 19
W 104–6: II 107 n 1, **113**
W 107: II 107 n 1, **113**, 123
W 108–111. II 107 n 1, **113**

www.ingramcontent.com/pod-product-compliance
Lightning Source LLC
Chambersburg PA
CBHW051105160426
43193CB00010B/1325